WHY DOES AUGUSTINE MATTER?

The Chadwick-Oden Lectures

What can today's Christians learn from voices from the long history of the church in order to understand their faith in a disconnected, digitized, and divided world? This lecture series, supported by Fieldstead and Company (Irvine, California) and hosted by the Premonstratensian (Norbertine) St. Michael's Abbey (Silverado, California), was created in honor of Henry Chadwick and Thomas C. Oden and their leadership among the church and academy. Annual pairs of lectures by leading scholars and authors explore the historical and theological roots of Christianity. They apply ancient, patristic, and early medieval Judeo-Christian thought and expression that approach the faith, not simply as a collection of doctrines, but as a transformative way of life. Videos of the lecture series may be viewed at the website ChadwickOden.org.

1. *Why Does Augustine Matter?* by Rowan Williams (2023)
2. *Why Poetry in the Bible Matters*, by Robert Alter (2024)
3. *Theatrics in Patristic Preaching and Biblical Exposition*, by Paul M. Blowers (2025)

WHY DOES AUGUSTINE MATTER?

ROWAN WILLIAMS

These essays are based on lectures given at St. Michael's Abbey in Silverado, California, on January 21, 2023.

Copyright © 2025 by Rowan Williams, ICCS Press.

ICCS Press, 616 Prospect Street, New Haven, CT 06511 www.iccspress.com

All rights reserved. No part of this book may be reproduced in any form or by any electronic or mechanical means, including information storage and retrieval systems, without written permission from ICCS Press, except for the use of brief quotations in a book review.

Library of Congress Control Number:
2025941541

Publisher's Cataloging-in-Publication
(Provided by Cassidy Cataloguing Services, Inc.).

Names: Williams, Rowan, 1950- author. | St. Michael's Abbey (Silverado, Calif.), host institution.
Title: Why does Augustine matter? / Rowan Williams.
Description: New Haven, CT : ICCS Press, [2025] | Series: Chadwick-Oden lecture series. | "These essays are based on lectures given at S. Michael's Abbey in Silverado, California, on January 21, 2023."--Title page verso.
Identifiers: LCCN: 2025941541 | ISBN: 9781624280504 (paperback) | 9781624280511 (Amazon) | 978-624280535 (ePub)
Subjects: LCSH: Augustine, of Hippo, Saint, 354-430--Influence. | Augustine, of Hippo, Saint, 354-430. Confessiones. | Augustine, of Hippo, Saint, 354-430. De civitate Dei. | Fathers of the church. | Trinity--History of doctrines. | Memory. | Identity (Philosophical concept) | Christianity--Africa, North. | BISAC: RELIGION / Christian Theology / History. | RELIGION / Christianity / History.
Classification: LCC: BR65.A9 W55 2025 | DDC: 270.2092--dc23

ISBN: 978-1-62428-050-4 (PB); 978-1-62428-051-1 (Amazon)

CONTENTS

1. HOW TO TALK ABOUT YOURSELF   1
   Author-Audience Discussion   26
2. HOW TO TALK ABOUT YOUR SOCIETY   41
   Author-Audience Discussion   65

   Henry Chadwick and Thomas C. Oden   85
   St. Michael's Abbey   87

I
HOW TO TALK ABOUT YOURSELF

It is a wonderful achievement not only to have established this precious archive here, but also to have instituted these lectures in honor of two of the most remarkable ecumenical scholars of the last century. Henry Chadwick in particular I am proud to count as a friend, a father in God, an ideal after which to aspire. Thomas Oden I knew far less well, but he too was a beacon of inspiration in all kinds of ways throughout his long and diverse scholarly career. I approach these lectures in the spirit of John of Salisbury, in the twelfth century, who famously described his work as that of a pygmy standing on the shoulders of giants, as I take a deep breath to launch into speaking about a theologian, a philosopher, a man of God, a father in God, a teacher in the Spirit, whose stature is perhaps unique in the whole history of the Christian church, certainly in the West, a figure central in Henry Chadwick's theological vision and one whose work he illuminated with immense clarity and depth.

It used to be said that you could decide to be a scholar of St. Augustine, or you could decide to be a scholar of the early church in general—but not both. Henry, of course, proved this to be completely fallacious, since he was one of the most distinguished scholars of the entire field of early Christian studies as well as one of the most distinguished scholars of the work of St. Augustine. Anyone today addressing either patristic studies overall or Augustinian studies in particular will be painfully aware of just how sketchy and superficial their own knowledge is. Nonetheless, to put it plainly, talking about St. Augustine is a challenge and delight, and any excuse to do so is welcome; which is why I am pleased to offer these general reflections on why Augustine matters today. Why should we still be reading him? What has he got to say to the twenty-first century?

There are many areas in which one could elaborate on this, many ways in which we could find answers. But I have chosen two specific ways for thinking about his legacy: how we think about ourselves as human beings, and how we think about the society we're in. Augustine wrote so much on so many topics that it is hard to know where to start. But—following his own example in his *Confessions*—one very obvious place to begin is with the questions that he puts to himself about his knowledge of himself.

It is worth recalling for a moment how the *Confessions* came to be written, and what kind of book it is. In the mid-390s, Augustine is already a bishop—a man in his early forties with a very considerable reputation as a scholar and a controversialist. He is aware that there are many people who look back on his earlier career with slightly raised eyebrows, not only in regard to what many would have seen as an irregular private life, but in regard to a decidedly colorful theological past. His appointment as a bishop has caused these suspicions to be revived, and he is conscious of a need to explain his record. The fact is that he had spent ten years as at least a nominal member of a proscribed and illegal oriental sect, the Manicheans. And for some of the more unforgiving of his co-religionists, this was ample grounds for hostility. Had this bright young bishop ever really shaken off the toils of heresy? It is as if today somebody revealed the embarrassing fact that some promising young defender of the faith had not so long ago been a member of a revolutionary Marxist cell or a fundamentalist Islamist network. Not too surprising if people wonder: Has he really changed? Can we really trust him?

So Augustine writes an *apologia pro vita sua*, as another rather distinguished theologian would put it, a defense of his life. But what is so fascinating about the *Confessions* is that it is not just an autobiography, not even one like Newman's. The point comes clearly into focus if we ask who the *Confessions* is addressed to. His colleagues? His "public"? Yes, but above all to *God*. The *Confessions* is, in plain grammatical terms, a long prayer. It begins very simply and directly with a quote from Scripture, *Magnus es, Domine, et laudabilis valde*: "You are great, Lord, and truly to be praised" (Psalm 47). And he takes off from there. At every juncture in telling the story of himself, he turns to God to say, "I acknowledge that I am doing this in your presence. I am speaking to the world by speaking to you, because only in that way can I somehow expose the whole of myself. I often *do not know* what is or has been going on in me, but You, God, do know. And so the only way I can talk truthfully about myself is by talking to You, since You know more than I know about who I am." He puts it more eloquently and briefly in the opening words of book X, "may I know you, who know me."[1]

As we'll see shortly, what Augustine is saying to us in this is

---

[1]. Book X continues by elaborating on the impossibility of keeping secrets from God; by exposing himself as fully as he can to God's judgment, he exposes himself truthfully to the judgment of suspicious fellow Christians, hoping that they will be encouraged and helped. See *St Augustine: Confessions*, trans. with an introduction and notes by Henry Chadwick (Oxford: Oxford University Press, 1991), X.i.1–v.7 (pp. 179–83). All citations from *The Confessions* are from this translation.

that we only learn the truth about ourselves by keeping our eyes on God. There is no way in which we can somehow excavate the truth of who we are just by introspection; we need to be talking and listening to the One who knows us more than we know ourselves, so that even if we cannot capture the whole truth of who we are, we still put ourselves in the context of the reality in the light of which that truth may begin to appear more fully.

The *Confessions* is a long prayer, seeking to do exactly that; but it is also a kind of interrogation by Augustine of his own story. He looks back; an incident swims into focus, and he asks, "What was really going on there?"—as if for a moment the light picks out a scene in all its vividness. And he goes on to ask, "How did that contribute to bringing me where I am today?" It must have done so, because God's hand is at work in everything. But how? So he turns over his memories; he reexamines his feelings and his perceptions from the past—and leaves the question open. He does not simply say, "I had this experience, and here are the lessons I learned." He says rather, "I remember this encounter, this conversation, these tormenting uncertainties; and somehow or other it was all woven into the story that I'm now telling."

This is one of the most original and most striking features of the *Confessions,* the recognition that, as I tell my own story, I myself don't fully understand it. In the ancient world, there were people who wrote about their lives, but there was no one before Augustine who wrote with that mixture of uncertainty and profound trust in the ever-present hand of God about their story, the capacity to say, "I can't know how I came to be like this, but I can know in whose hands I am and shall be." As he says, "I will reveal not who I was, but what I have now come to be and what I continue to be."[2]

---

2. *Confessions* X.iv.6 (p. 182).

Part of the energy of the *Confessions* lies also in the way in which Augustine asks why it took him so long to understand what to many Christians will have seemed the obvious truth. He describes what led him into the Manichean heresy, and does so largely in terms of the well-meaning ineptitude of a lot of good Catholic clergy (and his good Catholic mother) responding, when he came to them with difficulties, by saying, in effect, "Don't bother your pretty little head about that." Augustine looked for answers to difficult questions and was not disposed to be very patient with those who told him that it wasn't really that difficult at all if he just stopped asking.

What was it then that held him back from returning to the faith of his family? The *Confessions* is absorbing largely because he spells out so fully the various ways in which what had seemed like a set of neat and satisfying answers to his problems began to crumble under the pressure of experience and reflection. The heretical system he'd adopted seemed to offer an intellectual and spiritual shortcut; but like all intellectual and spiritual shortcuts, it came with quite a lot of risks attached. More and more, Augustine wanted to say, "I need to sit with the real difficulties, with a sense of mystery, and a sense of humility, rather than looking for rapid answers, because the rapid answer will not reach the heart of the question." At the very center of the *Confessions*, therefore, especially between books VII and IX, we find a whole series of reminiscences and reflections on that period in his life when he was nearly there but not quite. It was a time when the Manichean system had begun to dissolve around him and lose its persuasive power; he'd seen through it, and he was beginning—with the help of some exposure to a more intellectually rich style of Christian thinking grounded in the Platonic tradition—to see that Catholic Christianity might be the way forward. And yet there was something standing between him and the acceptance of the truth which he could not overcome for himself. Especially in book VII of the *Confessions*, he lays out the way in which he came to confront that brick wall in his thinking and his contemplating. He explores this by recalling the ways in which he was at that time thinking about both God and himself.[3] This is what gives the seventh book of the *Confessions* its very special flavor (in the interests of full disclosure, I should confess that book VII of the *Confessions* was a set text that I taught for many years as a professor of theology, so that it is quite deeply ingrained). And what he does is to identify a very basic fallacy. He implies in *Confessions* VII that the problem was that his failure to know himself was the ground of his failure to know God.[4] As we find out later, the reverse is just as true: he does not know himself because he has not understood what it is to speak of God.

In effect, what he explains for us is that he had not yet realized that his deepest identity as a self or spirit or soul is not a *thing inside him*. It is certainly not one of these Real and Authentic Selves we are supposed to be so interested in these days, a set of given needs and rights and dispositions. For Augustine, the "true self" is a continuing, unfolding engagement with the unchanging truth of God. This self is a movement, an energy, a process, not a thing. As you read through book VII, you see Augustine very gradually coming to the recognition: "If I am not a thing, but an action, an energy, unfolding, then God likewise is not a thing, not an item among others that happens to be lying around in the world. God is an energy and an act, an unfolding reality, embracing and pervading absolutely all that is." As the book advances, you begin to see that this is the watershed real-

---

3. See in particular *Confessions* VI.i.1–11.3, v.7, xvii.23.
4. See, for example, *Confessions* VII.i.2 (p. 112): "I had no clear vision even of my own self. . . . I did not see that the mental power by which I formed these images does not occupy any space"—and so Augustine does not yet grasp what it really means to say that God is outside space and time.

ization: I am not a thing. There is no little creature sitting right inside me somewhere, a buried "true self" that I shall find if I excavate deeply enough. No, the whole process of my being and action, the life that I am, is being drawn out by the grace and the love and the invitation of an infinite action, which I am never going to get my mind around. This is the key recognition. It means that when I understand what is wrong in thinking about myself, what is wrong in what I take for granted, I begin to see what wrong things I have been taking for granted about God.

In book VII, then, Augustine is describing how he begins to see these things about the self and God; and on this basis, he begins to understand that what holds him back from making a commitment is not simply an intellectual difficulty. It lies deeper than that. To make a commitment, you have to make a surrender of a certain kind of fiction about yourself; and making a surrender is a different kind of task from solving a conceptual problem. As he so wonderfully says in one of the most unforgettable passages of the *Confessions*, "To possess my God, the humble Jesus, I was not yet humble enough."[5] He uses a vivid image, both luminous and grotesque, saying that his self-confidence and pride had inflated him to such an extent that it was as if his cheeks were so swollen that he could not open his eyes.[6] But when those eyes are opened, what they see, says Augustine, is Christ, prone at his feet—God who has cast himself down to the earth so as to meet us where we are. I must stop scanning the heavens for God. I have to come down, literally, down to earth, to meet God. I have to follow *God's movement into the very heart of all things* in humility and love. And when I do that—when I, so to speak, fall to the earth where the body of Christ is—then

---

5. *Confessions* VII.xviii.24 (p. 128).
6. *Confessions* VII.vii.11 (p. 120).

as the body of Christ rises, I will rise.⁷ It is undoubtedly one of the richest passages in the whole of Augustine's voluminous work, a key to so much of his thinking, a picture to which the reader returns again and again.

So Augustine gradually comes to the point where a commitment is indeed made. I shan't rehearse the familiar story of his final moment of conversion,⁸ since the crucial insight is what he has to say about the nature of the breakthrough by which he arrived on its threshold. But when he has got himself to the point of being baptized by St. Ambrose, and also to the point of reconciliation with his long-suffering and loyal mother (look at the wonderful description in book IX of his last meeting with his mother, where together they share a kind of ecstatic awareness of God in their togetherness, just before her death), he then does something rather bizarre in book X, stepping back, taking a deep breath and taking stock. He begins, as we have seen, with the prayer, "May I know you who know me"—may I know as also I am known, in St. Paul's words in I Corinthians 13. He is going to try and sum up for us some of what the search for self-knowledge amounts to. In book X, he addresses the question more deeply and systematically than he has done before. Having in his account of his own life established, to his satisfaction, that the problem with commitment and faith is not intellectual but existential, he then needs to step back and say, "So what then is it for me to know myself truthfully?" He states what again in the ancient world must have sounded a very strange principle, affirming in effect that I cannot grasp the totality of what I am. I cannot grasp the totality of what I am. *I am more than I can know.*⁹

---

7. "They [human beings] fall prostrate before this divine weakness which rises and lifts them up" (again, *Confessions* VII.xviii.24).
8. It can be found in *Confessions* VIII.xi.25–xii.30 (pp.150–54).
9. On this, see especially X.viii.12–ix.16 (pp. 185–88).

This is a key insight for him. It is not just, "I am more than I am able to express," though that is part of it. It's also that there genuinely is in me more than I can bring into consciousness, concepts, and ideas, more than I can bring into programs and plans. It is as if the deeper I go into myself, the more I am aware of something endlessly opening up within. In another of his memorable images, he talks in *Confessions* X.viii.13 about the great underground "caverns" of the memory. Long before Freud used the image of caving expeditions for the understanding of our interior life, Augustine points us to the deep opening within us of a darkness we cannot fathom at the root of our memory.

Typically he begins by asking, "What is memory about?" One thing he is consistently good at in the *Confessions* is taking what seems absolutely obvious and asking what we actually mean by the words we use, how precisely we use them. What is time? What is memory? What is the self? And in book X this is more than ever central to his enterprise. What is memory? Because he is so acutely observant of his own mental habits, he is able to give examples that still resonate very clearly, examples of everyday experiences that we seldom stop to interrogate. When I sing a song, I come to the end of one line and I confidently advance to the next: I "know" what's going to happen next. But am I *thinking* about what's going to happen now? No. Yet something reliably comes into focus, and the process continues seamlessly. Augustine has helped us see that knowing a piece of music, knowing how to sing, is a stranger affair than we might have realized.[10] Then there are the things that I know I "know," but I can't actually remember—the "it's on the tip of my tongue" phenomenon. I know I know, but I cannot actually bring it to mind.[11] And then there are the things that obtrude into our

---

10. This example is actually form a bit later in the *Confessions*, X.xxviii.38.
11. *Confessions* X.xix.28.

memories when we would much rather they didn't. "Where did that come from? I didn't know I knew that. I thought I'd forgotten that."

A lot of book X of the *Confessions* is a deep interrogation of this interior world, a caving expedition, that will make us more baffled about what is routinely going on in us. I am a mystery to myself. "I have become," says Augustine, "a problem to myself"; *mihi quaestio factus sum*.[12] I have become a question. It's rather like the famous French poet of the nineteenth century, who said, *Je suis un autre*, "I am somebody else." Augustine, as in so many things, got there first.

And in the memory, it seems, I carry the world. Here is the passage in which he lays that out most fully.

> This power of memory is great, very great, my God. It is a vast and infinite profundity. Who has plumbed its bottom? This power is that of my mind and is a natural endowment, but I myself cannot grasp the totality of what I am. Is the mind, then, too restricted to compass itself, so that we have to ask what is that element of itself which it fails to grasp? Surely that cannot be external to itself; it must be within the mind. How then can it fail to grasp it? This question moves me to great astonishment. Amazement grips me. People are moved to wonder by mountain peaks, by vast waves of the sea, by broad waterfalls on rivers, by the all-embracing extent of the ocean, by the revolutions of the stars. But in themselves they are uninterested. They experience no surprise that when I was speaking of all these things, I was not seeing them with my eyes. On the other hand, I would not have spoken of them unless the mountains and waves and rivers and stars (which I've seen) and the ocean (which I believe on the reports of others) I could see inwardly

---

12. *Confessions* X.xxxiii.50; cf vi.9, on questioning who and what I am.

with dimensions just as great as if I were actually looking at them outside my mind. Yet when I was seeing them, I was not absorbing them, in the act of seeing with my eyes. Nor are the actual objects present to me, but only their images. And I know by which bodily sense the thing became imprinted on my mind.

But these are not the only things carried by the vast capacity of my memory. Here also are all the skills acquired through the liberal arts which have not been forgotten. They are pushed into the background in some interior place—but it is not a place. In their case I carry not the images but the very skills themselves. For what literature is, what the art of dialectical debate is, how many sorts of questions there are—all that I know about these matters lies in my memory.[13]

Images of the whole world and the diversity of the world, and the skills I've learned, the habits I've interiorized—all this is memory, and all this makes up the mental life of human beings. To use a couple of very non-Augustinian instances, do I, when riding a bicycle or driving a car, consciously call to mind images of riding a bicycle or driving a car, do I represent to myself the procedures I must go through? No. But the memory in my body, my muscle memory, as we would now say, does it for me. How do I contain not only images but the skills and the habits that allow me to negotiate the mystery and diversity of this world?

Very much more could be said about book X of the *Confessions*, as well as book VII. But I hope the main lines are emerging. For Augustine, talking about "myself" is talking about something that is so much more than just an object on which I can fix a label. It's reflecting on that action, that process, by which I am what I am as time moves on. Somehow, this spiritual agency, which is at the heart of my existence, absorbs impres-

---

13. *Confessions* X.ix.15–16 (pp. 187–88).

sions, habits, knowledge, vision, and is able to realize, moment by moment, how they work. And I can't freeze it. I can't take a snapshot of it. I just have a glimpse into the dark cavern of all these processes or motions that are living and acting through me and in me.

But to return to the point we touched on earlier, if this is how the mind works, then something about the mind is bound to be more than just intellectual. This is where we move into another area on which Augustine has a great deal to say in the *Confessions*, but also in many other works. Very broadly, it's to do with the interaction and interrelation of knowing and *wanting*, knowing and desiring. When I know something, I actually enter into a relation with it. I don't simply capture a set of formulae and slot them away in some internal electronic file. I enter into a relation because there is something in what I'm coming to know that is completing me, that is feeding me and nourishing me. [14]

I want to live. And I want to know because I want to live. I don't want to know just so that I can be the best person at knowing there is. I want to live, I want to live in joy, and I want to live in truth. I want to be more real, I want to be more in tune with what is truly there, because it is that "truly there-ness" of reality that will actually feed me and allow me to grow in life. The alternative is to have lots and lots of bright ideas and no future. But the knowledge Augustine is talking about is knowledge with an open future, we might say. I'm establishing a relationship into which I go on growing.

Philosophers over the centuries have poured out a huge amount of effort and ink on the question of the relationship between knowledge and love, knowing and willing, intelligence

---

14. On this, see, for example, from Augustine's early work, *De musica* VI.5, and from the later work, *De Trinitate* XI.2–12, on the to-and-fro relation of knowledge and *appetitus*, eager seeking.

and desire, and so forth, and there is a vast literature on Augustine's treatment of these things. But what is central to what he is saying to us about this is—and here is a bold claim, if you like—that no knowledge is just disinterested. We want to know because we have an *investment* in knowing.[15] This does not mean at all that we can bend the world to our needs and preferences and abandon our answerability to truth, but it does mean that our efforts to acquire knowledge are bound up with our efforts to be more human, to be more alive. And therefore the interaction of coming to know and recognizing our investment in knowing, our interest, our desire, is important. There is an element of commitment and relationship in how we come to know.

This implies that, speaking about ourselves, we need to imagine ourselves not as knowing machines, busily processing bits of information. We need to go back to that basic recognition that we considered in regard to book VII of the *Confessions*: I am an "energy." I am a purposive process. I am something coming to life, coming to birth. And in that coming to life, coming to birth, desire and love have a key role. I know because I want and need to know. I'm hungry to live. This doesn't mean I come to know only what suits me. Augustine is very definitely not somebody who could be adopted as a patron saint for the "post-truth" society we're so familiar with these days; he asks, significantly, who actually *wants* to be deceived?[16] Have you ever met anybody who says, "I'd love to be wrong?" No, of course not, says Augustine: the whole of our mental life begins in a hunger for truth, for reality, because if we are deceived we're not free. Somebody is manipulating us, somebody has got a grip on us,

---

15. See, for example, *Contra academicos* II.iii.8.
16. See for example *Confessions* X.xxii.33: "I have met with many people who wished to deceive, none who wish to be deceived" (p. 199).

something is being kept from us, and so we're less free and less real.

But the real presence of knowledge is a growth into freedom, where we begin to see what is true, how that truth is absorbed by us and helps us to live. Interestingly, he has a passage in book VII of the *Confessions*, where he says (I paraphrase a little) that one of the aspects of sin is that we delude ourselves that when we sin, we're acting.[17] The truth is that when we sin, we are in fact *passive*; something or someone is pushing us around. To sin is not to be free. And thus sinfulness and not knowing the truth are bound up together. We sin partly because we cannot see what is in front of our noses; and at the same time, it is sin that prevents us seeing what is in front of our noses. This is the vicious circle that leaves us trapped in a world where we tell ourselves all kinds of flattering lies about ourselves and our liberties, and end up digging the hole deeper and deeper and deeper. Sin is never a great act of triumphant, liberated self-assertion. It is being at the mercy of forces and persons outside yourself.

There is a strong link between all these pervasive themes in the *Confessions* to which Augustine keeps returning. I am not a thing, not a lump of stuff, but a life, a form of energy, like God. I do not fully know what's going on in me, and am always exploring the dark interiority of my mind and self. There is more in me than I could imagine and I am connected with more things than I can believe to be the case. So it is a huge fallacy to suppose that there is some concept of myself that I can isolate and freeze or fix. And opening up to the truth of where I sit in the whole mystery of creation at large is part of the pathway to freedom because it is a way of opening up to truth. As I open up more and more to truth, I become more free, I become more

---

17. *Confessions* VII.iii.5 (p. 114).

genuinely active, instead of being manipulated and manipulable by anything and everyone around.[18]

I underline this because later on I hope to say a bit about Augustine and the social vision, for which these ideas are essentially important. We shall see how they apply when he thinks about society, as well as our own particular human lives. But there is also one deeper dimension, on which I've touched in passing, but that now needs to be foregrounded a little more clearly in thinking through what Augustine has to say about selfhood. It should be clear by now that to be a self is always to be in relation. We're not made as little atoms, billiard balls dropped into a great empty area. We are made as part of an interactive, interlocked world in which wisdom, divine wisdom, holds us together, acting upon, with, and for one another all the time. So it is important to recognize that, while Augustine is sometimes associated with a kind of focus on the individual in Christian tradition, we have to be very careful identifying what kind of individuality is in view. He certainly has a more vivid and rich concept of the individual subject than any other ancient writer, Christian or non-Christian. But it would be profoundly wrong to call him an "individualist." Our own unique identity is always connected with the world we're in; and more importantly, it is connected with God.

Augustine has much to say about this in the *Confessions*, and especially in the last few books, where he undertakes a brilliant and original reading of the opening chapters of the Book of Genesis. But it probably comes to the fore rather more in the great work of his maturity, a work that took him the best part of twenty years to write, his treatise on the Trinity. This remains

---

18. For a vivid recent discussion of Augustinian theology and the culture of manipulated desire that we inhabit, see Mark Clavier, *On Consumer Culture, Identity, the Church, and the Rhetorics of Delight* (London: T. and T. Clark, 2019).

one of the peaks of Christian theology across the ages, an extraordinarily innovative, patient, careful, complex, puzzled, and bold attempt to show how we might talk about God as three persons in one substance without talking nonsense.[19] There are indeed a good few moments in the *De Trinitate* when Augustine steps back and seems to ask, "Does that sound like nonsense? Let's try again and let's see if we can get these concepts a little bit more adjusted to one another; this has to make some sort of sense, because it makes *human* sense. It makes sense in terms of the goal I seek for myself as a human person, so there must be a way of finding language for it." Of his language in this work, he memorably says, in effect, "I am talking like this not so as to get it all straight, but so as not just to be dumb about it, not just to fall silent": *ne taceretur*.[20] We cannot simply give up; we may not get it definitively right, but it is unquestionably right—and exciting—to try.

In the *De Trinitate* Augustine picks up the analysis he has already sketched in the *Confessions* (and in other places) about what is going on inside us as humans. We saw that in in the *Confessions*, he has a lot to say about memory; but the full picture, one that becomes absolutely canonical for the next thousand years in Western Christianity, identifies the three kinds of action that make us human as *remembering, understanding, and wanting*; memory, intelligence, and will.[21]

In the work on the Trinity, he says that this gives us a little bit of a sense of what it might mean to say that we are created in

---

19. The finest modern overview is by Lewis Ayres, *Augustine and the Trinity* (Cambridge: Cambridge University Press, 2010).
20. *De Trinitate* V.ix.10.
21. *Confessions* XIII.xi.12 outlines how we might think of the human self in terms of "existence, knowledge and will" as a kind of "three-in-one" model; but it is only in the later books of the *De Trinitate* (especially VII to X) that he gives a full account of what it does and doesn't mean to use the threefold structure of human existence as an aid to understanding what we say about the Trinity.

the image and likeness of God, as we are told at the beginning of Genesis. Here we have a reality which is one and indivisible, my reality as a thinking, feeling, knowing being. It is three activities woven together, absolutely inseparably. And yet, remembering simply is not the same thing as understanding, willing is not the same thing as remembering. They are genuinely distinct activities, and yet they are absolutely bound together in unity, unimaginable without each other. So yes; you might say that our inner life is a little like God in that respect; if you want to say God is three in one, so, in a sense, are we.

Yes, says Augustine, but we are missing something essential here.[22] Say, for the sake of argument, that God is indeed three in one—remembering, understanding, and willing. But *what* does God remember and understand and will? Well, what *can* God remember and understand and will in eternity? God. God remembers God. God understands God. And God wants and loves God. God is indeed three kinds of inseparable but distinguishable life. But each of those kinds of eternal life has the divine life as its own object—God, you might say, "containing" God. The unfathomable depth and resource of divine life is present to God, present as God understands, as God sees and makes sense of what God is. And when that sense has been made, God loves the sense that has been made, and "wants" it, wants to be God, is content to be God. (I remember a Dominican friend of mine, many years ago, talking about some of these issues, though mostly in the light of Thomas Aquinas, rather than Augustine, and saying, thoughtfully, "It's important to remember that for Aquinas God absolutely loves being God. He's having a wonderful time."). So God remembers God-ness, understands God-ness, loves God-ness, the Godly way of being

---

22. The following attempts to summarize the argument of books XIV and XV of the *De Trinitate*.

real. And the God-ness that God understands, remembers, wants, is real only in that interrelation. You may have to wait for St. Thomas to make complete sense of this; but that is another story.

But what about us? Surely, says Augustine, if we are really in the image of God, it is not just that we remember ourselves and understand ourselves and love ourselves. We are fully in the image of God when we remember God and we understand God and we love God. So our threefold life is *nothing in itself,* but everything when it relates to God. Somewhere in the middle of our complex humanity is this threefold capacity for relating to God. And the point of the life of grace, mercy, and healing, the point of the redemption that comes through Christ, and the life of the church, the body of Christ, is that this deep capacity, frozen or distorted in us by sin, is set free, and we come to share the divine life precisely by being liberated to remember God, understand God, and love God, so that God is the true and proper object of all the activity going on within us. It is then that we are fully in the image of God.[23]

Augustine, then, is not looking for the image of God in us by searching for correspondences between us and God—as if we could simply say, "The following applies to God, the following applies also to us, and there is a satisfying degree of correspondence between the two." He allows that this will clear up one or two possible problems (like the apparent outlandishness of speaking about unity in plurality), but in itself it is colossally misleading in that it suggests that I and God are two things within the same framework. Think harder about what you are saying about God, and what opens up is an awareness that we become completely ourselves only in relation to God, when we are taken into the life of God and see that this life is what makes

---

23. See, for a clear statement of this, *De Trinitate* XIV.viii.11.

us alive. We have no real life, no real knowing, nor even any real love, unless God is our object.

Here is another paradox that Augustine insists upon. If it is true that we only really become ourselves and only really know and love when it is God we're knowing and loving, then it is only because we know and love God that we can really make sense of anything at all. Once more, there is a vast literature on Augustine's discussions of whether God is necessary for our knowledge, whether we have to know God in order to know anything. Some of the great figures of Augustinian scholarship in the twentieth century, especially in France in the 1930s, clashed deafeningly over some of these issues; the details are for another context.[24] But I think it is fair to say that what Augustine wants to reinforce for us is the recognition that seeing things truthfully must at some level be bound up with God being the ultimate horizon of our minds; we know things less truly if we fail to see them in relation to God.

One of those great French scholars, Jean-Marie Le Blond, author of a very fine book called *Les conversions de saint Augustin* (The Conversions of Saint Augustine),[25] has insightful things to say about how, if we love the created world without reference to God, we are not really loving the created world at all. If all our love and all our attention is fixated on the world we are in, then in fact we do not actually see the world we are in. We are treating the world we are in as the end of all our inquiry and all our desire—and only God can be that. We confuse the world with God by making it all-important. Remember what was said earlier about not wanting to be deceived: warning lights should be flashing if we allow ourselves to settle down with such a

---

24. Ronald H. Nash, *The Light of the Mind: St Augustine's Theory of Knowledge* (Lexington: University of Kentucky Press, 1969), remains a clear introduction to some of these debates.
25. Jean-Marie Le Blond, *Les conversions de saint Augustin* (Paris: Aubier, 1950).

picture of the world. If we invest all our hope, all our love, all our energy in the world we are in, the projects we treasure— even, hard as this sounds, in the people we love—we are in danger of seeing them for what they are not. To see them in the hand of God, in the light of God, is to see them for what they are. So if our minds are open to remembering and understanding and loving God, then anything else we remember, understand, or love is going to make sense and to be seen justly as well as lovingly, in a way it will not be without such a context.

It is another of those large, "broad-brush" insights that Augustine approaches in different ways, with different wordings, at various points in his writing, returning to it as if to say to his readers, "Remember that? Another way in might be this." Because he is a copious writer and seldom a systematic one, the careless reader may often be held up wondering where exactly Augustine said this or that; insights and phrases recur, like musical themes in a symphony. But this specific insight about the knowledge of God and the knowledge of the truth of the created world can once again be tracked to some passages in the *Confessions*.

In the fourth book,[26] he writes movingly about a traumatic experience in his earlier years, when he had just begun teaching rhetoric in his hometown, the loss of his closest friend. The passage is full of the most extraordinary psychological insight; you could set it alongside Freud's famous essay "Mourning and Melancholia," or indeed, Jean-Paul Sartre's reflection on absence, and it will be clear how much Augustine foreshadows so many of the most influential and creative intellectual movements of modernity. When his friend dies, Augustine says, his devastated grief means that he senses the friend's absence everywhere (the experience of absence that Sartre discusses, or indeed the experi-

---

26. *Confessions* IV.iv.7–vii.12.

ence that is unforgettably described by Queen Constance in Shakespeare's *King John*—"Grief fills the room up of my absent child"). Augustine is all the time aware of the friend-shaped gap in the places where they spent time together in conversation and companionship. He feels it as a present privation for him, a loss of his own "substance." But at this point he turns on himself to ask who exactly is being mourned for here, his friend or himself. It is not the friend, it is the injured and diminished self. Augustine recognizes that he has invested too much in this friendship—not in loving too intensely, but in loving in a distorted way, treating the friend as the sole reality that could meet his deepest needs. And this is to treat a created being as God; so that when the friend disappears, the world collapses. Hence the grief is grief for the lost and disoriented self; it is not after all a sign of authentic love, because an authentic love would see the other person, the loved person, as related to God, not only to myself. So this remarkable section of the *Confessions* can be read as fleshing out the more complex theoretical perspective of the later work on the Trinity: our love must grow to the point where God is its destination—not God *rather than*, God in competition with, other things, but God as that to which all things relate and lead us.

He sums this up in the *Confessions* in another deeply memorable phrase, saying that he had failed to love his friend "humanly," *humaniter*.[27] He has failed to love his friend for what he truly was, a mortal and limited human being. This is—to make the point again—not saying that he simply loved him "too much"; it is about taking the friend out of the whole context of the real world and investing everything in him, making him all in all. But this is to project onto human beings what they cannot bear, forgetting your own solidarity with them in their limitation.

---

27. *Confessions* IV.vii.12.

Loving "humanly" entails risk, the risk of profound loss; but the greater risk is to invest in a person, a cause, a vision, with a level of absoluteness that belongs only to God. One of the essential things about a truly "faith-full" worldview is the recognition that when I encounter another human story, I look into a story in which God has already been at work; just as, when I look into the material world around, I see—not the kind of supermarket shelf of free or cheap resources that our modern civilization seems to think of, with all its appallingly familiar results—but a world in which God's life and love are already invested. I am always "coming late" to the other person or to the world around, because they are related to God before they are related to me. This, I suspect, is close to the heart of what a "religious" view of the world must entail.

Augustine is very seldom referred to as an authority in relation to the ecological crisis we presently face. But the fundamental weight and force of his theology should bring us up short if we are ever tempted to regard the world around as just such a supermarket of free resources as we have mentioned. This is a world in which God is already alive, and the person I love is one in whom God is already alive—which means that their meaning and the depth of their unique humanity do not consist entirely in their relation to me or their capacity to meet my needs. It is a clear illustration of how apparently abstract and complex notions such as we find in the treatise on the Trinity and elsewhere turn out to have real purchase on how we live with one another, how we live in the world we share. So much of what Augustine has to say to us about how we think of our humanity is contained in that much misunderstood and maligned word, *humility*. Being humble in the sense in which Augustine uses the term is essentially being *truthful*, in that it requires us simply to acknowledge what we are—to know ourselves, not exactly in a psychological sense, but to know ourselves as the *kind* of beings

HOW TO TALK ABOUT YOURSELF

we actually are—limited, time-bound, fragile, completely dependent on the utterly free action of God. This acknowledgment is literally the beginning of wisdom. Going back to the text of *Confessions* book VII, this means that there is a dimension of our spiritual life which always has to be a "coming-down-to-earth," a return to where and what we physically and concretely are. What is required of us is a deep, selflessly loving attention to what is real, because we believe in a God who comes down to earth, who embodies just such attention in living a timebound, vulnerable life for us; a God, moreover, who in Jesus Christ takes on the full cost, the burden and pain, the effect of our failure and rebellion, identifying with us so completely that, standing exactly where we stand—on earth, in the midst of confusion and guilt and refusal—the divine life is able to raise up humanity from within; not by magic, by a sovereign word from outside, but from what W. H. Auden called our "crooked heart."[28]

Another of the great poets of our age, T. S. Eliot—no stranger to the writings of Augustine—wrote of "the wisdom of humility," adding, "Humility is endless";[29] a good epigraph for Augustine's own perspective. We have to learn to be creatures, learn to know and to celebrate that we do not know and are not in control. The good news, it has been said, as I occasionally put it from the pulpit, the good news is that we do not have to be God. God alone is God; the job is taken.

And not being God is one of the key insights of Augustine's whole theology. As an older man, embittered and beleaguered in controversy, he was to insist on the sovereign grace and liberty of God to such an extent that you might be tempted to question whether, in some of the works of his last years, the vision of human dignity and human flourishing that he outlines in his

---

28. W. H. Auden, "As I Walked Out One Evening," l. 56.
29. T. S. Eliot, "East Coker," l. 99.

earlier writings has begun to wear thin. But this is not the whole truth. He spent long years locked in controversy with Pelagius, the austere British moralist, and with the bright young Italian bishop Julian of Eclanum, in those later years; and the recurrent theme, especially of his debates with Julian, is that, Augustine is saying, the world of moralists like Pelagius and celebrants of human liberty like Julian is unrecognizable to anyone who has looked into the reality of a human heart tortured by compulsions and betrayals. In one powerful comment he challenges Pelagius's assumption that all sin is direct "contempt of God." No, Augustine responds: some sins are indeed committed in pride but some "are obviously committed by people who don't know what they are doing, some by people who are simply weak, some—a great many—by people weeping and groaning."[30] The world of his opponents is too easy.[31] Yes, we are wonderfully made in the image of God, we flourish and grow into the glory of our adoption as God's children in the community of God's love, learning to look on the world with acceptance and gratitude. Yet, day by day, the habit of self-regard and self-protection remains deeply ingrained, the addictive lure of what we know to be bad for us is overwhelming, impossible to overcome by the action of our own will. Only the act of God breaking open the crust that has formed over our spiritual energies will set us free. The ingrained nature of our destructive compulsions becomes itself almost a compulsive theme for the older Augustine, in his angry impatience with both moralistic severity and bland optimism; and he deserves some sympathy here, even if it is hard to go along with all his conclusions. There are passages in those last works, especially about predestination, that are chilling; but they are so

---

30. *De natura et gratia* 33.
31. This is brought out very powerfully in Peter Brown's classic biography of Augustine, *Augustine of Hippo* (London: Faber, 1967), especially chapters 31 and 32.

partly because he looks around at the human world and says: "Tell me what good news can be derived from human achievement alone; look around you." He points to war, plague, tragedy, the deaths of children and the indignities of old age, asking, in effect, "Do you think that this is how it's meant to be? Is there no crisis to resolve, no prison to be broken open?" This is a terrible world precisely because it is, in the purpose of God, a wonderful world; if we celebrate its wonder without confronting the damage it suffers, above all the damage of our own destructive self-obsessions, we are lethally in error. Augustine is never someone who in any way relishes the harshness of the world's conditions or the apparent inevitability of human sin; he looks at the tragic realities of our life with a painful clarity, and insists that a mind or heart that truly knows God will lament as well as praise—and will be all the more astonished by the grace God offers.

If, then, we attempt the impossible and try to sum up what the saint has to say to us about how we know or think about ourselves, we could do worse than start with this blend of astonishment and lament. Augustine directs us to the deep caverns within us, where the act of God lies in the very depths, inviting us to discover or be discovered by it: he meditates on the mystery of our addiction to the unreal, to an unreal self in an unreal world, to a kind of loving that never truly engages with what is truly there before us. He reminds us that we know how to see only when we have a hint of seeing God in and through all, seeing the world in relation to its maker. And in knowing God, we do not seek a picture or an idea at arm's length, but the knowledge of our immersion in a divine life in which eternal perceiving and understanding and loving makes itself the foundation of all that is in the finite universe.[32] Into this mystery we continually grow, our life expanding into the depths of divine life and drawing up more and more from this well. Augustine's is a world in which we learn to talk about ourselves in the light of the awe and wonder that overtakes us in the presence of God's own light and life. This above all is what he has to teach us for today and tomorrow.

AUTHOR-AUDIENCE DISCUSSION

FATHER AMBROSE: Thank you so very much, Your Grace, for this wonderful dipping into some of the great masterpieces of our holy father, St. Augustine, and showing us how we can understand something more about ourselves and our place in the world, with his wisdom and his guidance.

I'm sure there are some questions, and we have some ample time for questions.

AUDIENCE MEMBER: Yes, thank you. Yes, I really appreciate what you were saying about the faculties of the soul in knowing. That is, memory, intelligence, and will. I lean more toward emotions, intellect, and imagination. And I was wondering where imagination might fall in play there.

I was also interested, very fascinated or encouraged by the knowing aspect, that St. Augustine says that you know something because you're invested in it. As you read a biography, you're starting to know this person. And as a Catholic, when we talk about knowing Our Lady or knowing a saint, and praying for their intercession, Protestants say, "What do you mean by that?

---

32. *Confessions* VII.xx.26 stresses that understanding the mystery of god is "not merely . . . an end to be perceived but . . . a realm to live in" (p. 130).

What do you mean you 'know the Mother of God'? What does that mean?" And so I've attempted to try to unpack that. It looks like St. Augustine could help me in that regard, quite a bit.

So my question is: where does imagination fit into what you were talking about, and what does it mean to know, when it comes to the saints?

ROWAN WILLIAMS: Thank you. I think the problem with "imagination," as a word, is that the sense we give to it is mostly a post-eighteenth century one. We've developed, thanks to some of the German tradition—Schelling or Goethe—and in English, Coleridge and his progeny, a sense of the imagination as a kind of powerful, synthesizing, adventurous element in our intellectual life, something a bit different from what we usually think of as "intellectual" activity. And rightly so for the most part.

But it's then very difficult to know what's the word in St. Augustine that might correspond to that. I don't quite have an answer, because I think that probably, for premodern thinkers, very often, "imagination" and "intellect" were not quite as detachable as they are for us. The very word *intellect*, as St. Thomas reminds us, is bound up with the idea of *getting inside something*, which is, I think, for many of us, the essence of an "imaginative" exercise, isn't it? It's a sort of constructing in our minds and to some extent our feelings, what it might be like to be there rather than here. And that, I think, is the bridge between intellect and imagination. When Augustine writes about *intellectus*, I don't think he's ruling out that kind of element.

So I think there are bridges to be built there, let's say. Having said that, as a kind of footnote, I would add that Augustine is very much in Plato's succession, in being a bit suspicious of some kinds of artwork because he's very wary of the way in which our emotions can be engaged uncontrollably or unconstructively. He thinks back to himself as a teenager, sobbing at the theater, at the passions of Dido and Aeneas, or whatever. And he says, I'm not sure I want to be at the mercy of my feelings in that way. He writes wonderfully, in book X of the *Confessions*, about music, again saying, I really feel I've got to keep an eye on myself when I listen to music because it takes me where I'm not really on top of things any longer. I'm not really in control.

But I think if I had the chance of a long conversation with Augustine—please, God, one day—I might want to say: "You give us this wonderful picture of what a humanity might be like that has in some ways *relinquished* control. Could you think of allowing that the arts have a benign, rather than just a manipulative role there?" And I think a lot of people want to pursue it in that way.

But then, to your second question, I love the idea of how we know the lives, the reality of the saints. I would say that when I think of relationship with the saints, I might want to go particularly to a specific saint because there is something about the contour or the rhythm of their life which feeds me. I know I need *that* unique and particular perspective on God at *this* moment—just as in our own ordinary relationships, we sometimes need to go and experience the company of somebody in particular because we're hungry for that particular perspective. We know that in this situation it would really help to talk to so-and-so because of where they come from and who they are. And I think that applies in the community of the saints, doesn't it?

I've got a large icon of St. Seraphim, the nineteenth-century Russian saint, in my upstairs prayer room at home. And I've felt for many years—like a lot of people—that Seraphim of Sarov is exactly the person I need around at all sorts of times. I know there's a kind of resonance and affinity—not that I have mysterious access to what was going on in St. Seraphim's mind or heart, but that there is a distinctive kind of witness here that I know need to be in touch with.

And when we think about prayer to the Mother of God, of course one of the things that's developed over centuries in thinking about Our Lady is surely—it happens when we pray the rosary—that we think about the *different* moments and dimensions of her life. Again, we sort-of-know because at one moment what she stands for in our minds is, let's say, the experience of loss at the crucifixion; and there's another when what she stands for and embodies is fruition and thanksgiving; moments where what she embodies is solidarity with the crucified Christ and with all those who suffer; moments when she is in solidarity with our joys. And so we know, if that makes sense, something of Our Lady's life because we see her in those moments exemplifying what it might be to have all these diverse emotions in the presence of Christ. And so we know that her prayer for us and with us makes sense in that context—if that makes some sort of sense to you. A really interesting question.

AUDIENCE MEMBER: I appreciated how you intimated some of the changes that a young Augustine had, and some fundamental convictions that remained with the late Augustine. Robert Markus speaks of Augustine as providing a defense of Christian mediocrity. I wonder if you agree.

ROWAN WILLIAMS: Thank you—and thank you for the reference to Robert Markus, once again a great friend and intellectual hero. The very first article I wrote on St. Augustine, back in the 1980s, was inspired by Robert Markus. And I remember sending him an offprint and writing on the top, "To my master," because he taught me such a lot.

Yes, a defense of Christian mediocrity. This is really the Augustine of the sermons, isn't it, but also the Augustine of the controversy with Pelagius. Pelagius has an undeservedly good press these days because people think he is some kind of liberal defender of freedom and democracy and all the rest of it. Pelagius is an impressive figure in some ways, but he's a passionate, fanatical moralist. Pelagius tells you that you are free to do whatever you like—so if you get it wrong, *it's all your fault*. Don't tell me that's good news. He is part of that intense ascetical movement that was so much in evidence in the late fourth, early fifth century, where there could easily creep in a belief that if you tried hard enough to live with extreme austerity, all would be well.

And Augustine looks at this and responds almost with a "where do I start?" Remember that quotation about sinners weeping and groaning as they sin. Sin is more like addiction than anything else. Hence, sin isn't freedom. But the point of that is my sin is not my deliberate, bold refusal of God. My sin is as often as not a kind of uncomfortable, burrowing, wincing, squirming incapacity, lack of nerve, lack of courage, lack of trust, lack of love, heading for my self-made comfort zone. Not very impressive, really. Likewise, my sanctity, my holiness, my virtue, is not my triumphant overcoming of all the obstacles, in Pelagius's style. It's just, "Thank God, God loves me." That's all I need to know.

Now, mediocrity. Augustine is preaching, day by day, week by week to the average person in Carthage. There is a wonderful article by Gerald Bonner, yet another of the great "fathers" for modern students of the fathers of the church, describing Augustine's typical congregation in Carthage. He says that you have to imagine crowded, sweaty churches (he has a wonderful note reminding us that people who live in a North African climate and wear a lot of wool will undoubtedly smell a bit overwhelming in church). They're jostling together while Augustine is sitting on his chair at the front, improvising as he speaks to them— speaking to the person who, rather like his own father, will probably come home drunk a couple of nights in the week, may beat his wife and servants from time to time, and not be entirely faithful. All right, says Augustine. We're not going to get *you* to heaven in a hurry, but here is what you can start with. So listen to this. Don't despair. Trust God. Make some resolutions. You'll fail. OK. Never mind. Start again. In Samuel Beckett's famous phrase, "Try. Fail. Try again. Fail better." That's very much the Augustine of the sermons. And anyone who has ever read Augustine's sermons will recognize this style— they were, of course, taken down as he delivered them, taken down in shorthand. You hear a distinctive, very human voice, a tired, realistic, compassionate but also quite steely pastor coming through. Don't try to be a hero, because if you try to be a hero, you will end up trusting your own resources in a way that is absolutely bound to let you down.

There is a sense in which Augustine, as he grows older, brings Christian mediocrity more into focus. The young Augustine has just been converted. He's ambitious and idealistic about what philosophy can do for us. He's going off for a long reading party in the country with clever intellectual friends, and they talk philosophy all day long. It's great fun.

He has never quite let go of that sense of intellectual exuberance. But more and more, as a pastor and a bishop, he says, Don't think that your Christian life is a walk in the park. Don't think that it's something which you're going to be in charge of, that you will be able to put temptation behind you. Trust, trust, trust. Love, love, love. And the famous, often misused statement, "Love and do what you like," which Augustine articulates in one of his late letters, doesn't mean what it sounds like it means. He's saying: Look. Struggle to let God make you a loving person. And then you'll be surprised what you want. You may find yourself not actually wanting to sin in the same way. "Doing what you like" is a bit different if you've spent years on the five-finger exercises of discipline and charity. But that's the level at which you start.

AUDIENCE MEMBER: Thanks for being here. I appreciate it. As a Presbyterian minister, I particularly appreciate the hospitality of a Catholic-Protestant setting here. It's really beautiful.

I was particularly struck with your mentioning of memory, intelligence, and willing, and how it became canonical for the next thousand years in Western theology. I discovered it in Augustine, and then Aquinas, and then [Bernard] Lonergan, particularly, in a great book, *Insight*. And to me, it still stands as this great treasure of a public-facing, humanist Christian theology of these internal experiences of remembering, understanding, and willing, in this connection with God.

Can you just say a little bit about what caused it to fall out of favor, and then what it might look like? In my circles, I experience it all the time, sitting among other Protestants who don't even know it exists. And our theological anthropology as Protestants is so poor. And then I will sit in Catholic circles, and it's a lot of intra-Augustine, Thomas conversations.

But what's really interesting and promising to me about it is that it can be this public-facing, humanist theology. And so anything that comes to mind about what it would mean to recover it for us, today?

ROWAN WILLIAMS: Thank you. Again, a really interesting question. I'm not sure I've got a quick answer to what put it out of favor, but I could make two rough suggestions. One is, of

HOW TO TALK ABOUT YOURSELF

course, that by 1500 or so, the fascination with classical antiquity, or rather a sort of fictionalized classical antiquity, had perhaps rather shifted off-center the great mainstream Christian anthropology that had developed in the way you describe.

And a different kind of picture of the soul—strangely, a rather less interesting, less nuanced picture—was emerging, and, along with that, a rather more narrowly intellectualist account of knowledge, which by the end of the seventeenth century, has begun to generate the Enlightenment and its legacy, which we are still living with.

So perhaps something of that is going on. If you put side by side with that the absorption of the Reformers in the agenda of the absolute sovereignty of grace—a very Augustinian theme, of course—it's as if suddenly Luther (Calvin a bit less so) allows the sovereignty of grace almost to steamroller any kind of nuanced account of what's going on in us. Because there's an element of Luther which says, "Well what does it matter what's going on in us? Because God is God, and God will do what God likes, and it's none of your business what God does."

(Calvin, curiously, is much closer to Aquinas on many matters than Luther is. And one of my minor intellectual crusades is trying to persuade people that Calvin is the nearest thing in the Protestant world of his day to a kind of reviver of St. Thomas and of the Greek Fathers. It sounds unlikely, but actually you can document it.)

But I think the combination of that rather simplified view of the classical world on the soul and the body, and its models of knowledge, plus a theology in which the analysis of what's going on in us becomes less interesting doesn't help. So it's fascinating that one of the most suggestive and creative uses of the triad of memory, understanding, and will in the sixteenth century, comes in the contemplative writings of St. John of the Cross—not in any systematic theology. He is the one who really picks up that tradition and runs with it, in the mid-sixteenth century, doing extraordinary and original things with it. John of the Cross has another imaginative stage beyond Augustine, saying we can map memory, understanding, and will onto hope, faith, and love. Faith is where understanding is heading, hope is where memory ends up, will is directed ultimately to love. And for St. John of the Cross, the whole arc of Christian experience is our capacity for memory, understanding, and love being transformed by grace into our renewal in hope, faith, and charity.

So there's one "Augustinian" development in the sixteenth century, just to remind us that it doesn't all go underground at that point. But it's significant it comes from someone who wants to look at the contemplative experience and how that works.

AUDIENCE MEMBER: Yes, my question is concerning actual grace. So it seems that the inspiration for knowledge is often an offering of actual grace from God. Would you say—and to which, of course, we may or may not respond appropriately—would you say it always is?

ROWAN WILLIAMS: In some sense, I would. We should say, I think, that we know because we're *invited* to know. Now one can perhaps build that up in stages. But we're in a world where because we're growing and moving in time, we have to know. We have to learn. And the circumstances in which we find ourselves, the regularity, the beauty, the order, and the challenge of the world, are, if you like, God's invitation to us to discover. We are going to cope better with the world we're in as we're invited deeper into this process.

But as we know more, we know it *at another level*. A very early hominid might know from bitter experience that it's not a good idea to put your hand in a fire. But at some future stage, they might think: Fire sort of changes the texture of things. What if we put this lump of soggy grain in some sort of a surface over a fire? What do you know? Bread (or toast).

And then, at another level, the reality, the complexity and beauty of another person invites us to a knowledge at quite another level of discovery, reward, delight in love. So yes, perhaps grace—in the broadest possible sense of God giving God's own Self into the world in wisdom and beauty—is always drawing us.

And this gracious, gratuitous gift of God in creation is always prompting us. Now, one can go beyond that, I think, in using the word *grace* in the slightly more technical sense, that we quite properly give it sometimes, and say there is grace in the sense that God invites us to know what we need to know for our heavenly, as well as our earthly, well-being. But I think it's on a spectrum, rather than just something isolated.

AUDIENCE MEMBER: It's clear that the all-pervasive model or analogy of intellect, memory, and will is there, and that's reflected on in all of Augustine's thought, and particularly in considering the *Confessions* and the *De Trinitate*. But it occurs to me—and I'd like your comment on this—that the secret of understanding the *Confessions* may be not in the psychological model, but in Augustine's struggle with the body and with his understanding of the nature of spirituality, as opposed to corporeality, and his struggles with his concupiscence and his real conversion is to that, to chastity. That's what really concludes the process, as it were, for his baptism.

But also, his conception of the scriptures with this totally literalistic, face-value view of the scriptures that he got from his mother in North Africa, and discovers the spiritual sense with

Ambrose that seems to pervade the different stages of his experience as a sinner, as a convert, as a preacher. And it's summed up, ultimately, in what you mentioned, the Word of God lying before us in humility.

So I think that Augustine is as much a preacher of the importance of corporeality, properly understood in the light of the Incarnation, "Lord, you struck my heart with your Word, and I loved You. And I can see by the Holy Spirit." He ends the *Confessions* with that kind of thing. I'm just thinking that's a point that maybe someone could pick up and make more of, in light of the psychological model. It's a comment, that I'd love to hear what you have to say about it.

ROWAN WILLIAMS: That's really helpful. Thank you. Yes, you're quite right. In a way, one of the themes that holds the *Confessions* together, which makes sense of those last books, when we think about Genesis, is the notion that we start with a faulty notion of corporeality. We start with a completely crude and unhelpful polarity between body and spirit, which ends up with, as he says, a materialist version of spirit itself. Manicheism. And we've got to get back to the idea that the life of the body is a meaningful life, a communicative life, therefore a life under discipline, a life which has a "grammar" to it, a logic that includes bodily chastity. And hence, also, the material text of Scripture is not just a flat description of what happened. It is an active communication of what God is doing now, in your intellectual—and indeed imaginative—response to the subtext, which is life and grace.

So yes, quite understandably, as Augustine finishes off the *Confessions*, he's demonstrating that there is a way of reading the Bible which gets you out of that sterile polarization of literal and metaphorical, material versus spiritual: the body (including the "body" of the biblical text) is what it is because it is suffused by, animated by, and ordered by, soul, spirit, God. That is what and how it *speaks*.

AUDIENCE MEMBER: Could you tell us about your prayer room?

ROWAN WILLIAMS: Simply a corner of the attic, in our rather small house in South Wales, where some of the icons that matter most to me, representing the saints who matter most to me, are propped up against the wall. And there is a cushion in the middle, where I do what I do, and sit and, I hope, receive.

It does matter to me quite a lot that there is somewhere in the house that is marked off for looking and listening, and nothing else. OK, it's one end of an attic, and the other end, bookshelves and desk. But in that corner, that's what happens, and it's there for the mornings.

AUDIENCE MEMBER: So in thinking of us as a mystery, and thinking of God as mystery, or the mystery of God. And it's no surprise that we are, I think, as you were saying, that we're made in the image and likeness of God. So of course, God is mystery.

I thought it might be interesting to talk a little bit about mystery as a closed door versus an open door, or versus an invitation because sometimes when someone doesn't have an answer, they say, "Oh, it's a mystery." And that's meant to end the conversation.

ROWAN WILLIAMS: Yes.

AUDIENCE MEMBER: But I think about the apostle, and I forget if it was Nathaniel or which one, where they said to Jesus, "Lord, where do you live?" And in a way, they were saying, we want to go deeper into the mystery. And He says, "Come and see." If someone tells me they don't really feel they know me, I say, "Well hang around more." And I just thought, as open door versus closed door, you might enjoy going at that.

ROWAN WILLIAMS: That's so helpful. Thank you. I was preaching on that text just a couple of weeks ago, actually, and precisely that theme of "Where do you live? Come and see. And they stayed with him." That's it.

"Mystery" can be what a friend of mine mischievously used to call a "tight-corner strategy"—oh, it's a great mystery, don't ask questions. But it can also more like: "Well, this is going to take a while. How long have you got?" Give it the time it takes to see the scale of what you're talking about. And if you think you've got it sorted—think again. Augustine says this plainly in his treatise on the Trinity: if you think you've understood it, it isn't God.

Now I take that as an open-door thing. He's not saying, stop thinking. He's saying, whatever you think, there is going to be more to think. Whatever you love, there is going to be more to love. And at the very end of *The City of God*, he seems to suggest that although we shall "rest" in heaven, we somehow go on seeing and expanding in vision. Growing and exploring.

So yes, I just think that puts it so helpfully, that "mystery" is about closed doors and open doors—and about how sometimes the church appeals to mystery to close things down when what we ought to be doing is appealing to mystery to open things up.

I think one of the most significant things we can ever say to our culture as Christians is: You know what? Human beings are so much more interesting than you think. You haven't begun to see the half of it yet. Sometimes when we tell the stories of the saints, that's a way of saying, human beings can be like *that*, amazingly.

When we talk about evangelizing strategies, for my money, this is the way in, saying: let me tell you about this kind of life, and leave you to ask: where does that come from? That's the open door, I hope.

AUDIENCE MEMBER: Thank you very much, Your Grace. It's clear to me and I think all the men in white back here, that you love our holy father, St. Augustine, and that his spirit really, you're imbibed with his spirit. And many of us back here are studying for the priesthood. We're studying philosophy and theology, and the works of our holy father.

So I just wonder if you have some words for us, encouragement in our studies. And secondarily, what made you fall in love with St. Augustine? What were some sort of influential books or writers that you read?

ROWAN WILLIAMS: Thank you. Well, a word of encouragement to start, then. Sometimes when I'm asked for "words of encouragement" from theological students and those on their way to the priesthood, the first and most important thing that comes to my mind is: never forget that the church exists, not because we want it to, but because God wants it to. And that means that the church lives because God wants it to. Our successes and our failures come and go. But the One who calls is faithful, as it says in Scripture. That's where, in the ups and downs of not only the priestly life, but the whole life of discipleship, it's absolutely essential to believe in God and to believe the church is only because God is.

About six months after I first became a bishop, I remember one of my clergy, a very loveable and impressive pastor, said to me, "What do you think you've learned, Father, in your first six months of being a bishop?" And I thought for a minute. I said, "Well, I suppose it's the absolute necessity of believing in God."

So for what it's worth—because we can so often give way to a kind of paralyzing anxiety about the church, since we live at a time when the church is riven with controversy, with polarizations, with the politicization of issues and sometimes also the trivialization of issues—we need that great advent cry, "Lift up your eyes and look. Your salvation draws nigh"—because God is God. When we are bogged down in those controversies and difficulties, we must keep looking at the God who chooses that the Body of Christ should exist on earth.

I was teaching at a seminary in the 1970s where, on the bell that called students to chapel, the Greek words were engraved, *pistos ho kalōn,* "the one who calls us is faithful." So whenever you heard that bell, you'd have that in mind.

Briefly, why did I fall in love with St. Augustine? I think it was probably when I was in my third year as an undergraduate student of theology, writing the routine required essay on the Pelagian controversy, just reading Augustine's responses to Pelagius. Given what we said earlier about how the older Augustine is not always at his most attractive, I still found that it was those moments of luminous spiritual insight and pastoral compassion woven together that made me know I had to spend time with this man. And I have, and I'm glad.

2
HOW TO TALK ABOUT YOUR SOCIETY

The bad news is that Augustine has no *theory* of society as such, let alone a theory of the state, or of "church-state relations." What he does have is something more comprehensive: not so much a theory, but a theology of human community. The fullest treatment is in his great work *The City of God*, and it is this text on which I shall mostly be concentrating in what follows.

It is worth mentioning in passing that Augustine is a model pastor in his capacity to adapt his language to specific and diverse audiences. In the *Confessions*, he writes a very distinctive, rather musical or rhythmical, prose in which he makes extensive use of the Latin Psalms—a style very well-adapted for meditative reading, reinforcing the prayerful direction in which the text as a whole moves. In his sermons, as we noted in the first lecture, he is speaking extempore; what we hear is the voice in which he would have addressed his large and mixed congregation, a voice that can be conversational but also intense, poetic at times but also blunt in its exhortations. In the work on the Trinity, he echoes the style of some Eastern Christian Fathers, finding a fresh theological voice to interrogate with patience and humility the meaning of terms and formulae against the background of Scripture and Christian practice, speaking to fellow thinkers in the Christian fold. But in *The City of God*, he reminds us that he can also write solid classical prose of a standard to impress a non-Christian intellectual audience—which is a very significant part of what he is setting out to do in *The City of God*.

In this work, he is making an ambitious pitch to those who are still—even after the official Christianizing of the Roman Empire—to some extent committed to the pagan mindset for which Rome, its rituals, its culture, its ethos, was the focus of religious loyalty. Some (not many, but including the man who had been the patron of the younger Augustine, the formidable senator Symmachus, who died a few years before Augustine began this book) believed that the Christianizing of the empire had been a disastrous mistake, that the gods had consequently abandoned Rome and given it over to the barbarians.[1] When, in 410, the Gothic troops of Alaric captured and sacked the city, such people—Christians among them—would understandably feel that the last days had arrived, and that divine protection for their society had come to an end. Augustine's response, written in the resonant and elegant Ciceronian prose of a classically trained orator, is to say, in a nutshell: "Empires come and go, cities rise and fall, but the community of God's people, God's 'commonwealth,' does not fail."

Not a theory of "church and state," then, but an investigation into the different rationales of human community, into the basic question of what makes a community durable, balanced, and life-giving. There were those in the Middle Ages, some Augustinian

---

1. Symmachus had, in 384, argued for the retention of the old Altar of Victories in the Roman Senate as a sign that the empire had not completely abandoned its ancient religious loyalties; see Peter Brown, *Augustine of Hippo* (London: Faber, 1967), p.70.

friars among them, who did their best (with varying success) to distill a full theory of the powers of the church and the powers of the state, the papacy and the monarchy, from his work.[2] But that was not his aim; what he seeks is to offer a critical and searching diagnosis of what habitually and systemically goes wrong in human community, and how and why the Body of Christ is the paradigm of human togetherness.

In a very celebrated passage near the end of book XIV of *The City of God*,[3] Augustine gives the most economical definition that he can provide of his subject matter, speaking of how two *civitates* (traditionally translated as "cities," but I'll come back in a moment to what *civitas* actually means), "earthly" and "heavenly," are constructed by two kinds of human love, a love of self that finally leads you to forget God and a love of God that finally leads you to forget self. Everything comes down finally to those two alternatives, every individual choice no less than every structure we create as societies.

But what exactly does he mean then by *civitas*? He is not talking about urban situations, about the distinctive kinds of behavioral and economic patterns that go with "city living." We translate *civitas* regularly as "city," but in the terminology of Roman imperial administration it stood for something much broader.[4] In Roman Britain, for example, the *civitas Silurum* was

---

2. Two great figures here are Giles of Rome at the end of the thirteenth century and his slightly younger contemporary James of Viterbo. Robert Markus's classic study, *Saeculum: History and Society in the Theology of St. Augustine* (Cambridge: Cambridge University Press, 1970), has a useful appendix (pp. 211-30) on how Augustine's ideas were radically transformed in this era to make them more compatible with the political perspectives of Aristotelian thought, especially in regard to whether all political power as such was—as Augustine took for granted —a kind of damage limitation for sin rather than a simply natural matter (as Aquinas believed).
3. *City of God* XIV.xxviii.
4. Cicero had defined the term as meaning any social group of individuals "contracted" to one another by agreed bonds and protocols.

the community, the tribal society, of the Silures who lived in my part of Wales. It is what other theorists might call a "polity," a structure of shared life and affiliation, with laws and traditions. It is not exactly an institution, more a shared cultural and legal environment for human life in common. And Augustine is arguing that such an environment will ultimately be shaped by one or other of the two kinds of loves he describes.

Augustine is, as we have noted, intending to address (and impress) an educated and residually pagan audience, the sort of people who might easily be led to think that all the problems of the Roman world are essentially caused by the conversion of the empire to Christianity. He mounts a comprehensive counterargument, to the effect that all the problems of the Roman Empire are self-inflicted, because the empire, like all human empires, is based on a fundamentally self-destructive set of assumptions. He steps back here to appeal to the impeccable classical authority of Cicero, and the definitions that Cicero had proposed, more than four centuries earlier, in the last days of the Roman Republic, of the *res publica*, the "business of public affairs," the nature of community and its governance. Cicero had stipulated that a *populus*, an identifiable sociopolitical community, could be defined as a multiplicity of reasoning persons associated with one another by common law and—a difficult phrase to translate—"communion of *utilitas*," perhaps best rendered as "having tools, conventions, and services in common." A working society recognizes shared needs and develops means of securing the meeting of those needs.[5]

But, Augustine argues, there is a deeper level of unifying reality in a viable society; he offers a revision of Cicero's defini-

---

5. Augustine is using Cicero's treatise *De re publica* I.xxv for these definitions; he opens his own discussion in *City of God* II.xxi, where he treats Cicero's formulations at some length.

tion, proposing that a *populus*, a people, is the coming together of a "reasoning multitude," *multitudino rationalis*, associated by "concord and communion in what they *love*."[6] Cicero stresses common practice and common law; Augustine pushes further to the level of what we might call "common values" (though it is not in itself a particularly helpful term). What holds a community together in this perspective is caring about the same things—not the structures of society as such but what characters and behaviors people want to see; ultimately, what sort of humanity people want to encourage.

It is a question that keeps coming back in contemporary political discussions—or, rather, we keep coming back to the absence of a context where such a question can helpfully be asked. In so many styles of political debate these days, it becomes harder to articulate the question of where exactly we want to get to as a human community or what kind of people we want to be nourishing and educating. The whole of our educational system, our approaches to healthcare, a variety of legal controversies, and much more will display this reluctance or inability to ask about what sort of humanity we are nourishing.[7] But this is the fundamental question for Augustine. A *civitas*, a *populus*, a social unit that makes decisions and establishes common ways of doing things is going to be held together by what people care about. And this is Augustine's bridge into talking about the love of God and the love of self.

If you have a community in which what is common among its citizens is that they all care for their own well-being and safety,

---

6. Augustine returns in XIX.xxi to the issue of definition, repeating Cicero's formula and then, in XIX.24, proposing his own version in terms of a human group united in what it loves, cares about or "takes trouble over"(*diligit*).

7. Hence the renewed—if rather diffuse—interest in questions about "character" found in contemporary writers like David Brooks; see, e.g., *The Road to Character* (London: Penguin Books, 2016).

you will want a significant level of power over your own circumstances and protection against the encroachments of others or of the collectivity. But if this is the one thing you most deeply have in common with others, you might notice that there is a rather significant problem looming up. If what I have in common with you is that we both want to hold on to the power we need to keep us safe from each other, this is not a brilliant basis for a stable life together, since it begins from the premise that there can be no conversation in which we can both actively work at defining something that will be good for both of us, or that will be good for me only if it also good for you. Such a conversation would be one in which we identified things we both cared about so that we would naturally want to work and think together.

Augustine spends quite a lot of time and energy dismantling the notion that we could have a viable society in which everybody is effectively out for themselves. He points out that it is as if we recognize instinctively that there is something wrong with this, because we find ourselves trying to fill a gap by creating common motivational myths. We have to find ways in which we can make the collective reality work, devising some means of damage limitation for the ruthless competitiveness and rivalry that grow up in a society devoid of real common love or value. And, Augustine proposes, the two great strategies which self-oriented societies go for are these.[8]

First is the pursuit of reputation, what he calls *gloria*. If you deeply long to be admired by people around you, you can moderate your own selfishness and pursuit of satisfaction a little, restraining your more murderous and destructive impulses in

---

8. The following summarizes themes from *The City of God* V.xii–xx (on the pursuit of *gloria*) and I.xxix (on the projection of internal conflicts onto an external enemy).

working for the approval of other people. You may have a rapacious and unassuageable urge to be in charge of everything and everyone, but you are enough of a realist to know that there are quite a lot of other people around who are going to resist you in this; so you conciliate, you opt for the "soft power" of people's good opinion. You set out to be liked and admired.

In the *civitas terrena*, the "earthly" city that is created by self-love, there is a lot to be said for dangling in front of people the goal of reputation, *gloria* (you can even work to have a reputation for modesty and self-restraint). It is one thing that puts a powerful brake on the "war of all against all" that threatens. This allows Augustine to be distinctly scathing about aspects of classical Roman culture and its heroes. What are those great figures after? *Gloria*; they want the late classical equivalent of paparazzi at the door, paragraphs about them in the paper, "likes" on online media. They want to be loved and are even prepared to make impressive sacrifices in order to be loved; they restrain their more openly and dramatically selfish impulses out of an essentially selfish motivation.[9] So quite a lot of what is presented to us in classical literature as heroism, says Augustine, is actually a very sophisticated displacement of egotism. His educated pagan audience would no doubt have bridled at this, but he means them to take him very seriously.

But the second, and perhaps simpler and even more attractive option for keeping a self-obsessed society together is to displace internal problems on to the outsider. Whatever the problem is, it is *their* fault, and very strong bonds of solidarity can be created by this strategy. The great task here of a successful society is reliably and regularly to find the most useful scapegoats.

Once more, Augustine goes back to Roman history, recalling

---

9. *City of God* V.xvii–xviii.

the wars against Carthage—a time when the Roman Republic held together brilliantly because everybody hated Carthaginians. Augustine notes a detail from a Roman historian who observes that when the third war against Carthage began, there were those who said, "We should be careful not to destroy Carthage completely; we may need it again." Inside observers of the Roman Republic knew very well that so long as their own society was lethally divided and fragile, there would be a need for an enemy against whom everyone could unite. Augustine is the first political theorist in Western history to identify this scapegoat mechanism, and he does so with clarity and cutting irony, unsparingly setting out the contradictions at the heart of the classical Roman myth.[10] His ironies are just as relevant to the rhetoric of the Cold War, the nuclear standoff, the war against terror, the Russian campaign against Ukraine, or the Iranian demonization of the West; it is always worth asking how much is fueled by the need to stop people thinking about the internal sicknesses of their own societies.

Such are the problems of the earthly city, the *civitas terrena*. Damage limitation is always possible, but what you cannot do is to give that society an intrinsic, internal basis for coherence and sustainability. Not only is it not built to last, it is built not to last since it is built on rivalry, on incompatible egotistical ambition. You can limit the damage by refining the selfish goals of individuals (*gloria*), and you can manage internal risks by projection outward, identifying a scapegoat (including of course the "enemy within," the fifth column of alien subversives). What you cannot do is to create a principle of internal coherence and harmony without rethinking your basic doctrine of humanity. If you want

---

10. He notes in I.xxix the argument advanced by Scipio Nasica against the destruction of Carthage—that security from outside attacks is "an enemy to weak spirits," leading to social breakdown; inevitably, in Augustine's view, where there is no solid *internal* motivation toward peace and mutual respect.

to have a society that will be *sustainable*, you must be able to identify the positive goals you share, the goals in which what is good for one individual or group is bound up with what is good for all. There is the positive heart of Augustine's *City of God*—not just his negative assault on "classical" values, but the insistence on the need to discover common goals, common goods, something which is not just a matter of my safety, security, or welfare at your expense.

Augustine is always a realist about human beings; he is well aware that we are not going to get to the City of God overnight. Accordingly, he says at one point in book XIX of *The City of God*, that even the inept methods used by Roman society to secure some sort of cohesion may produce results that may be temporarily good, results that are "good, and God's good gifts."[11] In other words, if these tactics preserve society from breaking down, it may be better than nothing. Yet this is not good in itself and cannot be durable. Ultimately what it lacks is *justice*. In the competitive, individualist world of the "earthly city," there is no true justice, even if there may be very provisional and patchy stability. As elsewhere, he picks up the language of classical writers like Cicero about *ius*, justice or law; but—as Robert Markus who was mentioned earlier says—he gives it a distinctive new flavor by associating it with the biblical notion of righteousness, and "right relation" with both creation and creator.[12] In this context, Augustine has a very interesting discussion of the nature of classical Roman religion.[13] In Roman paganism, people pay respect to the gods of their tradition and indeed to the imperial authorities of pagan Rome. But this means that they are giving to idols, "divine" or human, the respect, love, and

---

11. *City of God* XIX.xxvi; trans. John Healey, ed. R. V. G. Tasker, 2 vols. (London: J. M. Dent; New York: E. P. Dutton, 1945), 2:265.
12. Markus, *Saeculum*, pp. 64–65.
13. *City of God* X.i–vi.

devotion that belong to God. They are giving idols what belongs to somebody else. And since the classical definition of justice is to give to anyone and everyone what is due to them, this is an *unjust* state of affairs. What God "deserves" to have is love and service, worship, the sacrifice of obedience. If you deny this to the true God and give it to human leaders or pagan deities whom Augustine regarded as demons, overgrown and malicious fairies, you are being unjust by giving away to someone what belongs to someone else. And this is a poor foundation for a just society.

Notice how Augustine hints here at the idea that our eucharistic practice in the church is the supreme instance of justice. In the Eucharist, we give to God what absolutely belongs to God, which is God: we "give" the incarnate Christ to God the Father in the prayer of the Eucharist as we once again bring ourselves into the presence and power of Christ's self-offering in life and death, and are taken up into the incarnate Christ's exercise of "justice" toward God the Father. God the Son gives God the Father what God the Father "deserves," Christ honors the Father as the Father should be honored; and this is the foundation of atonement, redemption.[14]

When we join in this sacrifice of praise, we become "just," we become integrated into the true, appropriate, life-giving relationship which the Son has with the Father. And to see the Holy Eucharist as an instance of justice, as the place where "justice is done" to the glory of the Father, is to grasp more deeply than ever how and why we may begin to "do justice" to created beings as well. All this of course relates closely to what we were thinking about earlier in terms of how we come to see creation clearly and truly in the light of God and to give it the love that is

---

14. *City of God* X.vi: the perfect sacrifice is the unconditional gift of self to God which is perfectly accomplished in Christ, who incorporates us into his Body and makes us an offering—so that in the Eucharist, the church itself is offered, in and by Christ.

appropriate to it (rather than, in one way or another, treating creatures as if they were God).

This, then, is one of the things that characterizes the City of God: this community, this polity, this structure of human togetherness, is one in which justice is practiced, a justice centered upon giving God what is God's due, and in the light of this, learning to give everything and everyone what is due to them. And this is where a notion of true *common interest* comes in. We have a genuine common task as human beings; our common humanity is emphatically not in the fact that we are all driven by the desire to maximize our individual advantage. This common task entails respecting creation for what it is and giving to everything and everyone what it is appropriate to give. Once more, recall what we were reflecting on in the first lecture: in the life of grace, we come to understand our connectedness with the world we are in, we come to see a truth about the world that our sinful self-obsessions habitually prevent us seeing, and we are set free for a life together that is not constantly derailed or undermined by rivalry and the violence that goes with it. We learn in this context a common loyalty, a common fidelity to the real world, a fidelity not to ourselves over against "them," but the fidelity of faith (if you'll excuse the awkward wording)—a *faithfulness* toward God and therefore to what God has actually made.

It is in this light that the Christian community can rightly be seen as the source and the standard of true *civic* virtue. It gives to people living in the political order a degree of freedom and responsibility that is embodied in an investment and involvement in the well-being of the neighbor. It undercuts the collective pride and self-satisfaction of pagan society. It constantly challenges the way in which appeals to heroism, to the passion for glory and the lust for conquest and control (*libido dominandi*, a favorite phrase of Augustine's),[15] push against the true grain of what we are made for and unsettle and derail the common life. In some ways, it is a truly subversive model of human society—not subversive of social order but subverting any notion of order that does not depend on justice in the widest sense. A difficult vision for the late classical world; but not exactly welcome in the environment of advanced capitalism either, or the world of totalitarianisms of left or right.

Augustine is famously critical of the idea of empire,[16] and he is so largely, once again, on the grounds of justice. Political communities seeking to extend control over other communities in the name of extending justice or order pose a real problem in Augustine's framework. In one of his most celebrated aphorisms, he says that human kingdoms, human states or political units, without justice are *magna latrocinia*, literally "large-scale thievery," highly organized robbery.[17] He implies that without some notion of what is due to God and creation, what is just and truthful for all, any self-styled political order boils down to a kind of "mafioso" ethos. Even at best you have only a simulacrum of honor and corporate loyalty that is enforced by violence and exclusive of strangers. What you do not have is civic virtue, the deep commitment to the good of the neighbor that comes from recognizing your absolute solidarity with that neighbor.

What constantly gets in the way of this becoming a reality for us is what we have noted as the *libido dominandi*, the lust for dominance, the hunger for control: an aspect of our rebellion

---

15. The term is introduced in in XIV.xv as one of the varieties of "lust," the passion for control that is bound to be frustrated when we are in a state of fundamental disobedience to God; we are doomed to become "disobedient to ourselves," i.e., we cannot order our bodies or destinies as we want, so constantly try to secure this by dominating others.
16. E.g., *City of God* IV.xv.
17. *City of God* IV.iv.

against reality, against the recognition of our dependence, our createdness, the recognition that we receive before we give. The *libido dominandi* is the urge to be the one who takes the initiative and makes the decisions for others. And if that is true of every citizen of a polity or a state, common life is deeply vulnerable and finally unsustainable.

Augustine turns to the Hebrew kingdoms as described in Scripture to find a model that can be set up against the classical Roman model.[18] In these kingdoms, what matters is very clearly justice, in its full sense. Why else does the kingdom exist, if not because God has called this people to obey the divine law and to manifest the divine order and right relation to the whole world. But if we ask why there is a Roman Empire, the answer is that a people who have never heard of divine law or common good are constantly struggling to keep this vast wobbling jelly of conflicting egotisms together by constant adventures in aggression and violent struggles for dominance. This is bound to be an irreparably unstable situation.

This contrast between the Hebrew and the Roman model is a pervasive element in the background of *The City of God*, as Augustine seeks to clarify more and more fully what the *civitas Dei*, the republic of God, the "polity" of God is here and now. It is certainly not simply identical with the visible church; there have been many debates about the nuances of this in Augustinian scholarship over the years, but it is clear that Augustine does not think that the visible church is straightforwardly the place where God's justice is plainly established beyond challenge.[19] The church, as he so often reminds us, is still a commu-

---

18. *City of God* IV.xxxiv: the Jewish kingdoms have victory and prosperity without placating any gods, so long as they remain faithful to the one God. There is a longer account of the history of the Hebrew kingdoms in books XVI and XVII.
19. *City of God* XX.9 is the fullest treatment of this issue; the church is the Kingdom of Christ, but here and now that kingdom still contains those who

nity of sinners—as we should know well, since we pray each day to be forgiven our debts or trespasses.[20] The church is a "mixed body"; it is affected by the habits and ethics of the earthly city.[21] We who are members of the City of God are also—in a kind of "Venn diagram" overlap—involved in the earthly city and we carry over into the visible life of the church the habits of our unredeemed humanity. This was no academic issue for Augustine: much of his own work as a bishop was colored by his struggles with a particularly vitriolic and unpleasant local schism in North Africa that had been fueled by debates about whether the church could cope with its own history of public failure and betrayal (not an academic issue today either, for that matter)—a subject to which we shall return. He has no illusions about the institution.

At the same time, he is most definitely not an advocate of an "invisible" church. If you want to know where the Kingdom of God is, look at the lives of the saints, the reality of holy people, individually and collectively, growing and witnessing within the public, tangible life of an historical community. From this point of view, there is a sense in which the church *is* the City of God: if you want to see the City of God at work, go and look at a congregation that contains holy people. Where is the Kingdom of God? In the local lives of Jack, Sylvia, Manuela, Otis, Gladys, Vijay . . . And of course, in the wider and universal perspective, for Augustine, in the lives of Our Lady and St. Peter, St. Andrew, St. John, and (very much so for Augustine) the great saints and martyrs of North Africa like Cyprian and Perpetua and Felicity.

---

offend against its ruler; it is in some sense a kingdom at war. The saints rule with Christ here and now, but the church as a whole looks to a future promise not yet realized.

20. This is a major theme in his writings against the Donatists; the point about the Pater Noster is found in his Letter 185.39 among other places, and the *De baptismo* develops the argument that the church on earth still contains sinners.

21. *De baptismo* IV.x ff.; xii.18 uses the "mixed body" (*corpus permixtum*) language.

The Kingdom is present in such people because God "reigns" in their lives.[22] The Kingdom of God both is and isn't the institution of the visible church. Augustine is not saying that what we really need is a purely "spiritual" community without visible form and structure, a community of people unknown to and unrecognizable to one another, joined only in a mysterious interiority. Nor is he saying that this institution is the Kingdom and should never be challenged to repent and be converted afresh. It is like the fabric of shot silk: look at it from one angle, and you see one color, one texture; look at it from another and everything changes. Or, in another kind of image, look at the images in a kaleidoscope, coming together into coherence and then slipping apart again.

Here is the subtlety and maturity of Augustine's doctrine of the church. He is striving to come to terms with both the reality and the elusiveness of corporate holiness in a human society that is also a divinely created society; we make best sense of this doctrine as a reflection on what it is to be a community that corporately and publicly offers the sacrifice of justice to God, yet is always composed of persons struggling to align themselves with that fundamental fact. As we have seen, Augustine doesn't have a theory of church and state in the modern sense but a theology of these two styles of common life—love of God to the point where your self stops mattering, love of self to the point where God stops mattering. Everything comes down to these alternatives; and a community may "embody" the reality of the City of God even as a fragile and failing reality because its fidelity to the offering of justice, to the eucharistic fact at its heart, always remains.

A couple of questions immediately arise. One with which Augustine was quite preoccupied has to do with the nature of

---

22. *City of God* XX.ix: the saints are *where* Christ reigns.

political leadership and authority. One thing Augustine certainly is not is an advocate of the "divine right" of monarchs. He is an advocate of the divine *calling* of monarchs, which is a rather different matter. In *The City of God* he has some interesting passages on two Roman rulers, Constantine and Theodosius[23]—Constantine, the first emperor to legalize the practice of Christian faith, Theodosius, who was responsible for making Christianity the official religion of the empire. As Robert Markus very importantly underlines in his study of Augustine's thinking about society,[24] what Augustine doesn't say about Constantine is as interesting as what he does say.

In the Greek world, at the other end of the Mediterranean, there had been theologians like Eusebius of Caesarea in the early fourth century who were quite convinced that Constantine was, even in the Christian context, almost a god on earth, the anointed and chosen of God. As God delegated power in heaven to the eternal Word, so the eternal Word delegated power on earth to the Roman emperor. Augustine does not adopt that neat and rather alarming model; he is polite about Constantine, but it is Theodosius whom he holds up as an example simply because he behaves as a baptized person should—not because he is absolutely committed to imposing Christianity on everybody, as he undoubtedly was, but because he is prepared to do public penance. Challenged by St. Ambrose of Milan after he had sanctioned a massacre in the city of Thessalonica, he accepts Ambrose's sentence of excommunication and publicly repents.

A truly Christian ruler is more like Theodosius than Constantine, because a Christian ruler has to be aware of the common good and to serve it; and where the ruler fails or

---

23. *City of God* V.xxiv-xxvi.
24. Markus, *Saeculum*, chapter 3, is a good guide to the contrasts between Augustine and some earlier (Eastern) Christian attitudes to imperial authority.

offends against justice, he must be able to acknowledge this failure and make reparation. The ruler must be *filius ecclesiae*, a son of the church; if he is not contemplating the *lex aeterna*, the eternal law of God, his own enforcement of law is going to be flawed and fractured in any number of ways. The subject may be obliged to disobey it in the name of God. But the ruler is trained by faith not to be afraid of sharing power and admitting failure, because this is what it means in practice to be a son or daughter of the church.[25]

The chapter in which Augustine explains what is proper to a Christian ruler (the chapter in which the reputation of Theodosius is discussed) helped to shape the template for later medieval material about what a Christian prince ought to be—the so-called "mirrors of princes" tradition. And although not a huge number of medieval princes seem to have taken it entirely to heart, it remained the case that those basic principles were woven into the idea of monarchy in Western Europe through the Middle Ages. A true Christian prince must be somebody who is willing to share power, who is willing to repent, who is willing to be challenged and held to account by a law that is higher than the ruler's own arbitrary will. Part of the task of the Christian community is to hold the ruler to account, and, where necessary, to refuse obedience to any law that actively promotes injustice.

Augustine is already beginning to lay the foundations for what in St. Thomas Aquinas becomes a complex and quite far-reaching theory of the rights of what we would now call civil disobedience, noncooperation with unjust law. He does not believe, any more than Aquinas does, that violent sedition and revolution are good things in themselves. But both leave room for a principled refusal to cooperate with an unjust system, a system that overrides the common good by its brutality or parti-

---

25. *City of God* V.xxvi.

sanship. Augustine as much as Aquinas stands behind the witness of an Óscar Romero or a Desmond Tutu in resisting and naming public injustice—but does not give any sanction to the idea that there's a kind of legitimate counterviolence, by which you can overthrow public injustice for good and all, and set up a guaranteed and unchallengeable religious government. There is no way of avoiding the need for vigilance, responsiveness to different crises and problems.

Augustine's *civitas Dei* is a *civitas peregrina*, a "society on a journey," a pilgrim society.[26] The church knows that, as a human and historical community, it has not yet arrived, it does not possess all answers and solve all problems. We are all still on a journey toward the fullness of love, knowledge, and reconciliation. There is a paradox here: the "earthly city" is always being undermined by its own inner disorder and trying to impose external order; the church knows its own human disorder in external matters but relies on the grace of God as a force that renews it internally from age to age. It is always in search of the freedom to realize the kind of power that gives itself away and shares itself, the kind of vision that nurtures common commitment to common good.

So in Augustine's perspective, "talking about society" is always talking about the church; not in the sense of gossiping about "church affairs," church politics, or whatever, not in the sense that our social program is simply making everyone docile members of the institution. But it is belonging in the church that gives us the tools for understanding social life, understanding what a communal, shared life looks like when it is just, orderly, and durable. The church in this sense is a touchstone for

---

26. The opening chapter of *The City of God* states clearly that this *civitas* is also "on pilgrimage" (*peregrinator*); it would have been a striking paradox for Roman readers, for whom the basic contrast in political rights was between "citizens" and "migrants," *peregrini*.

social life, clarifying for us what questions we should put to our representatives and rulers. It is not an ideal; its own manifestation of God's justice is patchy at best and often deeply scarred by failure, by prejudice, cowardice, idleness. (Why did it take centuries to wake up to the evils of slavery? Why did it collude with pre-Christian myths about the inequality of gender? Why did it default to self-protective mechanisms in the face of the most appalling patterns of abuse? And so on.) But the "Venn diagram" still applies. If you want to know what just, life-giving social reality looks like, that is what the church is for, and that is where the Kingdom is at work, in the midst of a bitterly compromised human history.

There are so many incidental insights in *The City of God* that would require more exploration and further elaboration than Augustine gives, but I shall mention just two which are especially striking. One is in a passage in book XIX of *City of God* where he says that if you live only in the earthly city and by its self-defeating values, you will never experience true *friendship*, because all you have is, ultimately, competition.[27] If you are locked into a model of acquisition, seeking security at each other's expense, how can you be friends? As so often, Augustine quarries his knowledge of the classical tradition from Aristotle through to Cicero, noting that this tradition treats friendship as an exchange of goods between equals. (We might look at the beautiful account in the *Confessions* of friendship as conversing easily, reading books together, doing small kindnesses for each other, sharing jokes together, disagreeing amicably.)[28] One question, then, that we might ask of any political vision is whether or not it makes friendship possible.

The second tangential point to mention is a brief observa-

---

27. *City of God* XIX.vii–viii.
28. *Confessions* IV.viii.13.

tion in book IV of *City of God*, where he says, in effect, that one of the problems about tyranny and oppression is that it is bad for the tyrant as well as the tyrannized.[29] One reason we should resist and oppose unjust and oppressive regimes is that they are sending unjust rulers to hell, not just creating hell on earth for those who are oppressed. To challenge a tyrant, a Vladimir Putin, a Kim Jong-un, or a Robert Mugabe, is among other things to show a concern for their soul.

A brief personal reminiscence here of meeting Robert Mugabe some years ago, for one of the longest and toughest hours of my life. The bishops of Zimbabwe had asked me to go and talk to him about human rights abuses in the country, especially the violence directed against some church personnel. I went with the Anglican archbishop of Southern Africa, the deeply impressive Thabo Makgoba; and when I had received the standard response that, as the representative of a racist and imperialist church, I had no business to tell the president anything at all, Archbishop Thabo weighed in and challenged the president as to how he could call himself a Christian and ignore these abuses. In that context, Archbishop Thabo could say what I couldn't; but it was a deeply "Augustinian" moment, illustrating how pushing back against oppression and injustice is ultimately for the sake of the oppressor as well as the oppressed.

Another Zimbabwean story, from the days of the civil war after independence (when Mugabe was responsible, as became clear over the years, for the slaughter of thousands of members of a rival tribal group), may be relevant. A leader of one of the most bloodthirsty militias had been apprehended by a group of peasants from a village in an area that had been ravaged by this militia and brought before the tribal court in the village. People had given evidence of the atrocities for which he had been

---

29. *City of God* IV.iii.

responsible in the area. At the end of it, the elders of the tribal court asked the militia commander what he thought was the punishment he deserved; he said that he assumed he would be killed. The elders replied that this was what they were not going to do precisely because it was what the commander would take for granted. Again, a profoundly Augustinian episode, one of those moments of "anarchic" Christian witness, impossible to systematize or codify, but unmistakable as a sign of the Kingdom, the *civitas Dei*.

Augustine notoriously developed a reluctant justification for the use of force in public affairs, a "just war" argument.[30] But we should pay as much attention to what he has to say about peace. He has much to say about how we balance the peace of the body and the peace of the soul, and how we need to seek physical, actual, practical peace for the soul's sake. We try to create peace and reconciliation in our world so that human beings may learn to love and know God and in consequence may be set free to be human in the way they are created to be.[31] This opening up of the possibility of peace in the soul—which is ultimately reconciliation with God—is how we assess the reality of any claim for peaceful or just settlement in the world: will this strategy, this project, set people free to be at peace with God? Once again, in our contemporary setting, Augustine offers not a schematic solution but the sort of questions that will bring discernment. The church cannot determine political policy, but it may probe and scrutinize, looking for what in any program might open the door more effectively to the peace of the spirit. It is not too far from Dorothy Day's insight that a state cannot make people virtuous

---

30. See *City of God* III.vii, XIX.10 for brief comments. The literature is large; W.R. Stevenson, *Christian Love and Just War: Moral Paradox and Political life in St. Augustine and His Modern Interpreters* (Macon, GA: Mercer University Press, 1987), is a helpful survey.

31. See, e.g., *City of God* XIX.xiv, xvii.

but it may make it a little easier to be good. If our society is not dominated and shaped in obvious ways by the Christian ethic, it may still be capable of securing the sorts of freedom that allow Christian persons and others to grow in the way they should.

A subtle distinction, perhaps, but one worth underlining. And part of its interest is that Augustine himself is by no means consistent in his own attitudes. A little earlier, we noted Augustine's involvement in handling a very bitter controversy in the North African church, the controversy with the "Donatist" group—an extremely influential and numerically very large body in the North African church, probably larger than what was recognized as the Catholic Church in North Africa for a significant period.[32] The key claim of the Donatists was that they had never compromised with the persecutions of the Roman Empire by handing over sacred documents to the imperial police. They had always been consistent—in marked contrast, so they claimed, to the Catholic bishops and leaders who had at times compromised their integrity. The precise rights and wrongs of all this were already, by Augustine's time, lost in the memory of the chaos and misery of the years of persecution, but the mythologies were alive and well. Both sides in fact seem to have had a tarnished record in some ways. By the time Augustine became a bishop, the division had solidified, and there was a good deal of violence between the two parties. Augustine himself received death threats, and at one point narrowly escaped death in an ambush by Donatist militants. Others were less fortunate. There were violent uprisings in some of the Donatist-dominated regions. Augustine began by repudiating the idea that anyone could be coerced into orthodoxy; but as the conflict continued,

---

32. The most comprehensive study remains W. H. C. Frend, *The Donatist Church: A Movement of Protest in Roman North Africa* (Oxford: Oxford University Press, 1952), though many of its conclusions would now be challenged.

he lost patience. He picks up the phrase which Jesus uses in one of his parables, "Compel them to come in," and—fatally—uses it to justify force against his opponents.[33] The Donatists are, he believes, cutting their own throats, and for their own good they must be compelled into the Catholic Church—and punished by the state if they resist.

Augustine certainly did not believe in executing heretics, but he did believe in legal sanctions against them, fines and imprisonment and exclusion from public life. Against the background of *The City of God*, it is not exactly what you might expect of him. Yet it is not impossible to understand in his context, a context which the great Augustinian scholar Peter Brown used to say was comparable to the religious conflicts in Ireland in the last century and a half, a landscape of savage sectarian brutality.[34] The tragedy is that in later centuries Augustine's extreme and impatient response became for many people the justification of a systematic policy of persecuting and executing heretics.

Augustine should not be judged only by that moment as we think about his political legacy. In his most deeply considered texts, what he is most deeply concerned with and committed to is the community of justice and love, the common good. As he says in his letters,[35] this true commonwealth, this society of shared good, depends on *faith*—both in the sense of belief, and in the sense of fidelity, a faithfulness to God the Creator, a faithfulness to God's creation, which accepts that my own definition of my interest and my agenda is not the last word on anything. I am (to recall the themes of the first lecture) already involved in more than I know, connected with more than I can see. My fate, my good, is bound up with all that lives around me, and whatever

---

33. See for example Letter 185.24.
34. Brown, *Augustine of Hippo*, p. 229.
35. Letters 137, 138.

I do in the public sphere must be done with this in mind. "With this in mind"—not that there is a rule book for politics here. Augustine will say to his friends in the civil service and the military that they must make their own decisions, but must do so in the light of the most serious attempt to begin with the love of God. In a much-quoted and much-misunderstood phrase,[36] he exhorts such people to "love and do what you will." This is not by any means a recommendation to a "situationist" ethic in which loving intentions overrule any specific ethical imperatives. It is not about doing what comes naturally. It might better be translated, "love God and do your best." Love God, try to want what God wants, and then perhaps you will not close the door to grace and mercy, and may find ways forward that will serve God's will.

The City of God is never a manifesto, nor is it a clear recommendation of which party to vote for and which policies you ought to be advancing in the public arena; it provides a set of key questions for Christian discernment: does this or that policy, this or that approach to the ordering of our life together liberate or constrain the possibility of growing into holiness? I mentioned Dorothy Day's comment on how the laws of society might make it slightly easier to be virtuous. In one way, this is the sum of an Augustinian politics; but it is crucial not to lose sight of the fundamental vision of the Body of Christ, the community on pilgrimage. The most important contribution that the City of God, the commonwealth of Christians, can make to the wider social unit is the clear recognition that there will never be a point where we can stop thinking, praying, and acting for justice —and so there will never be a point where we can stop interrogating and challenging our social habits and assumptions. We must go on being politically restless even in our spiritual peace-

---

36. *In Epistulam Ioannis ad Parthos* VII.viii.

fulness. We shall always be uncomfortable citizens. It was Karl Barth who said—after a distinguished record of making himself a thorn in the flesh of the Third Reich that—the Christian is always going to be a very unreliable ally in politics, because the Christian is never going to sign up uncritically to a definitive partisan package. The Christian will always have the awkward question to ask, because we are still on pilgrimage, not yet there.

What matters most in Augustine's perspective is the sense that the deepest question in our social life has to do with the two loves he describes. Are we, as a society, acting on the basis that we are atomized individuals, bound to love ourselves in a way that leads to forgetting God, or on the basis of something more? The church exists, not as the triumphant illustration of what things look like when all the problems are solved, but as the manifestation of what things look like when people turn to that deepest question and allow it to go on questioning them and enlarging their imaginations, moving them to repentance and renewed trust, seeking to live out a life in which we're not constantly at war with one another, individually or collectively. We are called, in this light, always to look for what it is that we can recognize as allowing us to flourish side by side under the God whose absolute love is extended to all of us—even more radically than Augustine himself recognized, perhaps. But this is at least part of how we might allow him to open up our thinking and talking about our confused and needy society in the twenty-first century.

AUTHOR-AUDIENCE DISCUSSION

AUDIENCE MEMBER: Thank you, Your Grace. It so joyful and enjoyable to have you walk us through these thoughts about these really seminal texts and these wonderful, wonderful and inspiring ideas. So thank you for the approach, and really it's like a journey that we're on together this morning and this afternoon, and that's a great blessing for us. Thank you.

I want to begin the question-and-answer period with a question pertinent to our life here. It's, of course, not without reason that we're speaking about St. Augustine in a monastery where we men are striving to follow the rule of St. Augustine. We're Augustinian Canons Regular, and I'm sure I was not alone in hearing you speak about the common project of striving for a shared love, for example, or trying not to dominate, one's desire to rule over one's brother, and so forth. All of these principles, these Augustinian principles upon which we build our monastic life here, and—or a marriage, that's right, what I hear from the front row. Sure. Family life is religious life and also family life, no? Absolutely.

But my question is: you've been speaking and having our holy father, St. Augustine, speak to us about society writ large and how we might look for the seeds of the Kingdom and struggle against that paganizing temptation toward self-assertion. Where do you think or, if you can maybe help us Norbertine Canons Regular, Augustinian Canons Regular, learn how our life, in this striving for the Kingdom here in the church as a kind of a witness to that, that the whole church and the whole world can look to, and maybe how he can speak to us in that?

ROWAN WILLIAMS: Thank you. A key question, thinking very specifically of your life under rule. I'll come back in a moment to how that applies to the church at large, but it certainly applies particularly to those living a vowed life, a life under rule. Of course, it's not just a life "under rule," it's a life in which the worship of God, the giving to God what is due to God, is utterly inseparable from what you're trying to do in the ordinary give-and-take of community. This is one of the things that strikes me about the monastic life in the most general sense, that it is not simply a project of living together as human beings. It's a project of praying together; and the project of praying together is, of course, one in which you can't ignore the reality that God is as interested in the person next to you as God is interested in you. And therefore—it's there in the rule of St. Benedict as well as in the rule of St. Augustine—the common life is one in which a deepened sense of the depth and value of each person comes into focus, in worship as well as in washing up, or whatever it may be, whatever common work there is.

So I would say that the witness of the vowed life in this connection is absolutely about the fusion of work and worship, the common life as expressed in the Benedictine tradition as the *opus Dei*, the job you do for God, which is prayer. Everything hangs together in this context. And I'd go on to say about the common life of the church in general, that it is important that we talk about and think about worship, not just ethics, here. If we try to live a life which witnesses to justice and liberation and all those important things, we do so because of how and what we worship. We don't just do it out of ethical obligation; and what so frequently draws people to the life of the church is not that we have an impeccable record of supporting good causes—we don't always, though there's nothing wrong with supporting good causes—but that we have the fundamental impulse of joyful offering to God at the heart of it. That's what makes the difference, that's what animates it all. And part of what we do, therefore, in terms of our evangelization, our outreach to the world, is, to put it rather bluntly, to look as if we know what we're doing when we're worshiping.

AUDIENCE MEMBER: Thank you so much. This is speaking our language as canons for sure. This is what we do, so thank you for that. Just one further thought by way of conversation. The beginning of the rule of St. Augustine speaks of our common project of striving for a unity of heart and mind on the way to God together, so that's that unity of purpose. At the very end of the rule, he says that we are striving to be, we are to treat each other, and the abbot is to treat us, as together we are lovers of spiritual beauty, the thing that we love together is spiritual beauty, God under that aspect, and so of course, when we're praying together, singing God's praises together, this is where we're nourishing that common love. So very encouraging, thank you for that.

AUDIENCE MEMBER: Thank you, Your Grace. I was wondering, we have been taught to meditate and to say that, during the Mass, the Eucharist is the sacramental re-presentation of the sacrifice of Christ at Calvary. He is really present, so I'm curious to hear your comments on that. Do you think that's a good way to describe it? Do you respect it? We are most eager to know.

ROWAN WILLIAMS: The brief answer is yes. That is, I think, exactly what the Eucharist is. It is our being drawn into the eternal self-offering of Christ to the Father, which is embodied —transformingly, uniquely—at Calvary. But the great Anglican monastic writer on the liturgy, Gregory Dix, used to say there is *one* coming of Christ. In eternity, the Son, as it were, "comes" to the Father in the eternal response of love. But that coming is also Christ's coming in the Incarnation and Christ's coming at the end of time and Christ's coming in the Mass. In eternity, they're all one action, they're all the action of Christ, Christ's love flowing toward the Father. But it's like a single beam of white light coming through a prism. It's broken up into different colored rays, and the Eucharist is one of those rays.

In the seventeenth-century Anglican tradition—which was, of course, very suspicious of a lot of medieval Catholic rhetoric about the sacrifice of the Mass, for reasons which I think I can understand—people came at this from a slightly different angle, saying that what happens in the Eucharist is to be thought of as a re-presentation of the heavenly priesthood of Christ. So there really is a participation here on earth in the life of the Christ who offers the world to God in eternity. There's a famous instance from an Anglican prayer book, of about 1630-something, that has a woodcut opposite the first page of the Holy Communion service. The top part of the image is Christ in heaven standing at the heavenly altar, and underneath is the priest at a Holy Communion service of the seventeenth-century Church of England—echoing the motion of Christ to the Father, the action of the heavenly High Priest. It is a re-presentation of this reality—not in the sense of an imitation at a distance, but a participation in a present and real action. And again, to do justice to some of the Reformation theologians, there's a lot of Calvin which points in the same direction. It's not a matter of just symbolizing an absent reality but of sharing a present reality. This is one of the big areas of ecumenical convergence in talking about Protestant and Catholic eucharistic theology—and it is certainly something which Henry Chadwick was very devoted to exploring.

AUDIENCE MEMBER: Your Grace, in a secularizing time which is growing, and is being taught to be skeptical of religious institutions, how can people of faith speak most effectively in enunciating Christian values in a way that lulls people into hearing them and unlocks what's best in the society?

ROWAN WILLIAMS: How indeed? Well, I mentioned this morning something about how our ability to tell good stories about where the Kingdom happens and what it looks like is part of this effective speaking. And I mentioned in the second lecture figures like Óscar Romero and Desmond Tutu and Dorothy Day. There'd be many others about whom we could say, "You want to know what this Christian language is really about? Let me tell you about so-and-so." Not just the big names, either, but the little ones: this is what it looks like. And we try against this background to sow the seed of the question, "What motivates people to live in that way?" That's where the door begins to be pushed open sometimes. It's not, I hope, a waste of time to do the fundamental digging over the intellectual soil in debate with the vocal atheists of our day, the Richard Dawkinses and all the others. How many atheists have Richard Dawkins's arguments made? Probably very, very few. But how many vaguely skeptical people has Richard Dawkins confirmed in their prejudices? Lots. So it is not a waste of time to try and sort out the intellectual tangles; but it's not the whole story. After all, it's not that people stop being Christians because the arguments stop working, or that people become Christians just because the arguments come alive. People stop being Christians very often because they can't see the transforming reality of grace in actual lives; and just as often they become Christians because they can. So how do we make that transformation visible?

You may have heard me say this before, but I've occasionally thought that we ought, at least in private, slightly to revise the creedal formula. "I believe in one, holy, catholic, and apostolic church," and change it to "I believe in one, holy, catholic, apostolic, and *repentant* church." Because our ability to admit that we're not there yet, that we have made mistakes and committed

HOW TO TALK ABOUT YOUR SOCIETY

sins, and we haven't "got it" is also something which has evangelistic potential and reality.

AUDIENCE MEMBER: Your Grace, could you say more about the outcome of the interview with Robert Mugabe? My wife and I served six years in Zimbabwe. We never had an hour with him, but you know, he addressed the World Council of Churches while we were there, and he would come to my parish and give long speeches, this sort of thing, and we weren't happy about a lot of the stuff that he was up to, his Cuban and North Korean buddies and all of that. Was there any outcome?

ROWAN WILLIAMS: Well, I'm not sure, but I think there was. Perhaps I can spend a moment on the background. What prompted the visit was partly the crisis over the then bishop of Harare, Nolbert Kunonga, a friend of Mugabe's who had benefited extensively from the regime, and was essentially running a reign of terror in his diocese, issuing threats of violence against his clergy and organizing gangs to go and beat up opponents in the parishes. Behavior that I think we can safely say is a step beyond the acceptable variations of episcopal ministry.

The other bishops in Zimbabwe had eventually said, after a couple of years when they had been begging me *not* to say anything so as not to worsen the political situation, "Now it's time to intervene. We are declaring Bishop Kunonga deposed and excommunicate, and we are electing another bishop for Harare, so now is the time to say something." So I did.

We were getting reports constantly at that time of what Kunonga and others were doing, reports about gross human rights abuses in the parishes and church institutions in Harare, as well as the general issue with Mugabe's rule. But of course, he was still protecting Bishop Kunonga at that point. Kunonga was accumulating lots of church property in Harare, sequestrating colleges and schools and properties belonging to the diocese for his own private profit.

During the conversation with President Mugabe, I referred to the crisis in the diocese and the record of human rights abuses; and when Mugabe said, "Well, I don't know anything about that," I was able to pick up the extensive dossier that I'd been given and say, "Well, you know now. There it all is, documented." My deputy chief of staff, who was with me in the meeting, said he thought he could identify the moment at which Mugabe was calculating: is it worth going on backing Bishop Kunonga, when all the bishops in this room are uncompromisingly against him? Three days after the visit, the Supreme Court in Harare gave its first verdict against Bishop Kunonga in a case about church property. So I think it may be that going with Archbishop Thabo and Bishop Chad of Harare and the others directly to the president had at least made Mugabe withdraw a few inches of his protection from Bishop Kunonga. Something in the climate of the church in Zimbabwe changed a little at that point, I think.

A small effect, perhaps. I like to think so. There's one other little anecdote that I can't resist relating here. Bishop Kunonga was absolutely determined to make our visit unpleasant, so he'd hired a lot of people to come and protest at every event I was speaking at. One day we went out to Penhalonga, a great Anglican mission station, which the monks of the Community of the Resurrection had run. It had been taken over by the pro-Kunonga party, and this great complex, a huge church, a school, a convent, was now surrounded by barbed wire. We arrived to visit, to make the point that we regarded this still as the church's property—and sure enough, there was a group of protesters with placards outside. Well, we climbed over the barbed wire, went up

HOW TO TALK ABOUT YOUR SOCIETY 73

to the church, said some prayers and sang some hymns; and then noticed—rather a surprise—that the people who had met us at the barbed wire fence with their placards had come to join us and were singing hymns with us. When pressed, they said, "Well, we've done what we were paid to do. We came, we demonstrated, so now we're very happy to join in."

AUDIENCE MEMBER: This kind of flows from the last lecture. So, that very interior reality that is going on in the *Confessions*, how does that bridge into the communal life? It seems like it's kind of the question of the philosophers. The modern philosophers are all about "me," and all about the interior, but then they completely lose the common good. So it seems like, even as you had said, the way to invite people into the church is to teach them, "Do you really want to live with a reality that's that small, compared with the interior world which the Christian has?" Nevertheless, it's very difficult to express that interior, because it's interior, so in what way does interiority become a common good?

ROWAN WILLIAMS: That's a really strong question, I think. I suspect it works a bit like this. One of the things which Augustine is trying to say in the *Confessions* is, the more you look inside, the more you see that there is (as I said this morning) no "thing" there. You exist as a self simply because God is giving to you, moment by moment. Without that, there's nothing there, and with it, you realize precisely that you are already connected. It is this sense of connection with the rest of God's world and connection with the will of God that makes the bridge into action. We are always already connected. We are not made as billiard balls. We are called into being as part of this system of justice and balance and interaction, which is creation. Unless you have that, there's a sort of void at the center of the world's reality. And if you do have that, then you understand that you are answerable to, bound up with, your neighbor, as St. Anthony of Egypt put it, "your life and your death are with your neighbor." That's what you discover.

You invite people to look inside; and either they ultimately discover they are loved by what they can't imagine or they discover there's nothing fixed or trustworthy there. It's a tough message, but I think that this is how you make the connection, when you have the chance to explore this kind of conversation. Is there or isn't there a primal act of love and calling?

Would you like to come back on that?

AUDIENCE MEMBER: Yes, just briefly, is there a way in which that expresses in life? So like, not just evangelization, because that's a first step, but is there a society which lives the internal experience communally?

ROWAN WILLIAMS: Well, yes. That's us. It's the church, it's the religious community, the parish, whatever, in which what you're doing, whether it's as a church in general or a religious community in particular, would make no sense without this belief that you were connected, that your life and your death were with each other. Part of what you're living out is the declaration that, yes, we care intensely about the inner life, about standing silently and adoringly before God, we care about it because this is what nourishes our sense of one another, what makes us care about one another and nourishes our sense of the need to go on standing before the mystery. That's exactly what's going on in the life of Christian community. It's bringing those realities together, living out that connection.

AUDIENCE MEMBER: I think it was G. K. Chesterton who said that the mark of the Christian is gratitude. And I was just thinking about what you said: you look inside and either there's nothing, or you see that God is loving you, and that would lead to gratitude, wouldn't it? It strikes me that in our age now, there's not a lot of gratitude floating around out there.

ROWAN WILLIAMS: Absolutely right; and what we must constantly ask is, does the church look grateful? Do we give the impression that we can barely contain our excitement at what we've been given? Don't hold your breath, you might say. But there ought to be *something* of that coming through, however inarticulately, something we can share with people.

The great Protestant theologian and martyr Dietrich Bonhoeffer famously said that a good sermon is like holding out a large red apple to a hungry child. This is good, this is life, we say; and we can convey something of that sense of thanksgiving (otherwise known as Eucharist, of course; just to make the connection yet again). Why, after all, is the Eucharist, the Mass at the heart of our corporate Christian life? Because it is where we're not only drawn up into the self-giving of Christ to the Father, but we are *defined* as the people who give thanks for this gift. That's who we are and what we are, nothing more, nothing less. At that moment, all we are as human beings is "beings who thank God." What a privilege, what a miracle, to be participants in the Eucharist. Just for that moment we are nothing but creatures giving thanks to God, in the Son, by the power of the Spirit, to the Father. Do we sound grateful? We have reason enough.

AUDIENCE MEMBER: Two questions, actually. One, what is love anyway, because growing up, I've gotten the impression that the Christian ideal of love is just wanting what's best for someone, which can, for a kid, mean that loving you means wanting you to eat your vegetables or wanting you to be punished, sometimes physically, and is therefore often rather unpleasant and depressing. And secondly, in regards to the Holy Community of God, I wonder if you could comment on the role of marriage, sex, family, in it, please. Thank you very much.

ROWAN WILLIAMS: A large agenda here about applying all this to marriage and sexuality. Let's see what we can do.

First of all, on love in general. Certainly for Augustine, love, *caritas*, is essentially, as you say, that complete commitment to the good of the other. It's a recognition that, for the other to flourish and to live is bound up with me flourishing and living. I want what is good for the other partly because it's good for me as well—not just as a kind of refined selfishness; but no one is simply "selfless" in the sense that their own life is something totally indifferent to them. I know that when my neighbor lives, I live, and I want life for both of us, for all.

Now, when I turn that into a policy that simply says, "But I know what is good for you, and I'm not going to listen to what you say is good for you," then we have a problem, and perhaps this is the problem you are reminding us about—because this is what the church rather habitually tends to do. I am absolutely committed to your good, and absolutely committed to your life, and I will tell you exactly what you need in order to live it. And so we can sometimes get into the position which has been described by somebody as "giving flawless answers to questions that nobody's asking." Be warned.

So there has to be a degree of sheer attentiveness in our love that seeks to reflect something of the deep attentiveness, the gaze, of God upon us; not to say, "Well, I know what's best for you," but, "I'm listening to see if we can find how we move in harmony." This is hard work. Love is, in this sense, very hard work. But this is how I would seek to avoid some of the real risk and danger that you've rightly identified, if I heard your question correctly.

On the broad questions of marriage and sexuality and so forth, that's another day's worth of talks at least, not only in relation to Augustine but more widely. Just a couple of very brief comments. Augustine is blamed for almost everything that has gone wrong in the church, not least for negative attitudes to the body and sexuality. Those who say this have probably not read enough of the church fathers, because Augustine is pretty mild by comparison. There's a wonderful passage in one of the discourses on the Epistles of John, where Augustine rather surprisingly says that the embraces of the marriage bed are one of the ways in which we anticipate the joys of the Kingdom. You don't quite expect this of Augustine, because in the *Confessions* he's so preoccupied with the recollection of his own failures. He is in many ways very typical of his time. We were reminded of this this morning, by Father Hugh: his own commitment to chastity in the *Confessions* is a focal theme because he's aware that he has abused and neglected a relationship. The pain of this comes through starkly in the *Confessions*. He both wants to put it all behind him, but not to refuse to look at it and think about his failure. We've seen that as he grows older, he gets fiercer in some respects; but he also grows milder in others, and he can say some remarkably positive things about ourselves as sexual beings.

But what worries him most about sex is the sense that it's not easily controllable, and here he is definitely a man of his intellectual time. As he says, most bits of our bodies act as they do because we want them to. But there is one particular area of our bodily lives which is notoriously unreliable, where the motions of the body don't follow the mind in any tidy way. He's afraid of the surge of irrational, instinctual, subhuman passion. He has undoubtedly recognized something true about human experience, though whether he has drawn the right conclusion in regarding sexual desire as so uniquely dangerous, I am less sure. Yet at the same time, he is capable of saying that there's something about the trust and friendship of committed sexual union in marriage that is absolutely valuable in the sight of God.

AUDIENCE MEMBER: Bishop Rowan, thank you so much for this talk, and I've appreciated the . . . appreciated how you pointed out various injustices that you have been a part of addressing, being present in addressing. I remember hearing theologian Jane Williams one time sort of point out that anything you acknowledge and identify as true, and I teach in the sociology department, anything you identify as true was a revelation of the character of God. She made that point. So maybe this comes back into a question about Eucharist, but I'm curious, and I'm having some of my students read as I mentioned to you, the German sociologist Hartmut Rosa, and sort of his notion of resonance, his theory, and the reading is a short book, *The Uncontrollability of the World*.

Now, you mentioned earlier, the ecological crisis, just in passing. And I wonder—come around to that, coming around to sort of how this affects political regimes around the world, and entities, local and larger—I wonder if you can comment on your own theory of social change, and how you might, you know, appreciate sort of looking at Augustine identifying demons. But it seems like you're also even potentially willing to work with those demons, you know, if they are willing to change, right, for the common good, or something like that. But how does your theory of social change work in such a way where it also would resist sort of modernist technologies of control, and those sort of desires?

ROWAN WILLIAMS: I'm not really sure I've got a theory of social change, but I have a few thoughts about it, which I'll try and share. Let's start with one point about social change which I think is important: *how* you bring about change affects *what* changes. A change that's brought about with one or another form of power-based or even technology-based control is going to be a vulnerable kind of change, and a potentially exclusive kind of change. If you're prepared to become more comprehensive and deep-rooted when it's made, that's a good thing; but this is not what people always want to hear, because people like instant change, and—as I think you are hinting—they like to borrow the language of technical control and mastery to justify shortcuts. So that's one point.

A second point: one of the really challenging elements in discourse around social change revolves around one word which seems to me to crystallize a lot of it. How does what I desire as change become *recognizable* to you in the change you also desire? How do we create mutual recognizability? Many of the standoffs in our world, especially in our "culture wars" environment, really discourage us from such searching for any kind of recognition—so that the person I disagree with can very easily be written off. I say, in effect, "What you want, what you think desirable, is clearly something so different from and so hostile to what I want that we can't talk." There may be contexts where we are genuinely driven to this; but meanwhile, can we just do a bit of work on this to ask what is recognizable across the frontiers *before* assuming the worst?

I remember somebody saying once in an interfaith event that, in discussions between Muslims and Christians, we discover that there are vanishingly few Muslims who want their children to have a miserable life, who want the planet to go to hell in a handcart, who want tyrannies to prevail across the world, and who want the traffic regulations that keep the local schools safe to be suspended. Well, this is a start. Vanishingly few people want manifestly destructive things, goals we absolutely can't recognize. Can we identify one or two of those in our discourse? Because if we can identify something of this, we have one way of handling what is sometimes called in political theory the issue of "loser's consent": "I've lost this argument, I've lost this election—so do I now have any stake at all in the new situation, anything that would make me want to go on managing to live with it?" If I've done a bit of this preparatory work of recognition, the question makes sense. I've lost. I'd much rather this government were not in power, but they are for the next few years; is there really nothing on which I can work with them? But if you set up every political, social, or moral conflict as a total collision of absolutes, then when the other side wins, you will easily feel you have lost *everything*, that you have nothing left to lose. What then? You have no stake, no future. What can you do? You can resist violently, you can refuse cooperation, you can work for the dissolution of the settlement. What you won't do is to find how you can move on to a constructive choice, and work toward the moment when you can reopen the argument.

I may not be putting that very clearly; but one of the things that worries me about our whole culture at the moment is that we are so committed to standoff and zero-sum modeling as the default setting in our public life. I'm not saying that there are no areas where the disagreement may be absolute. But remember:

very few people want actively destructive outcomes, and their motivation for their choices may not be so impenetrably alien as you think. This is connected a bit with something Augustine has quite a bit to say about. He is clear that sin is not and can't be directly *wanting* evil, because there's nothing there to want. You want good, but you want it in a distorted form or you want to arrive at it by a bizarre and stupid and self-destructive route. Nobody wants evil—any more than (as we noted this morning) anybody actually wants to be deceived. All this gives us something to work with, maybe. I'm not at all sure that this adds up to a theory of social change! But these are two things which are often in my mind as I think about the topic.

AUDIENCE MEMBER: It seems to me that so much of our language is imbued with the lust for domination. We often put things, it seems, in a way that expresses our desire for power, our desire to compel that kind of thing, in parenting, in marriage. I mean, I'm old enough to remember when we had the war between the sexes back in the sixties. They wrote books about it. They made comedies about it. It was a big thing. Now I think it has become a complete thing, a full-on. But at work, in the church, in reform, reform can sometimes be about winning and not really the good outcome. And I'm just looking at, how can we examine the way we communicate and start to purge terms of power out and make it in terms of gratitude? I mean, here we sometimes say, "Well, you have to go to Mass every Sunday," not: "You are privileged that you will be able to." You can go, and God offers you a gift, and you can pick that gift up as often as you like, you know. I'm a convert. When I go to Mass, the first thing I usually end up saying is, "Thank you for letting me be here," because to me it's a gift.

ROWAN WILLIAMS: Yes, that's lovely. One of the phrases I like most in one of our Anglican eucharistic prayers is when we thank God for allowing us "to stand in your presence and serve you." That's the point I hear you making, which I absolutely resonate with. I think I might just let that stand, because you've said so much there (and I'm losing my voice!).

AUDIENCE MEMBER: Thank you very much, Your Grace, for speaking very many things to muse upon, and I appreciate your wisdom. It seems like, in our age, we are very scared of authority, and we tend to reject most and all authority that is put over us. So what does Augustine have to teach us about delineating between authority and speaking with dominance, because a just authority figure certainly speaks with a power over us, so . . .

ROWAN WILLIAMS: Yes, a variation on how do we handle power, and how do we avoid the seductions of power? A lot of it has to do with how authority makes itself accountable—by which I don't mean filling in forms and all the rest of it. But it's important, I think, in any ecclesiastical community, to know that your pastor, your abbot, or your bishop, whoever, is someone who makes themselves accountable to others, goes to confession, takes counsel, exposes the processes of decision making for challenge. It's interesting, in the rule of St. Benedict, that although the abbot's power is delineated in pretty stark terms, nonetheless, it's the abbot's job to go around listening, not least to the youngest in the community, who, says Benedict, may have something to say you wouldn't have expected.

So some of this is about how that authority becomes credible by being transparent in its operation. I can recall in the work of a diocesan bishop, moments where in taking a decision you had to find a way of saying: "Look, I think I'm going to have to do something that will be difficult or costly for you. I would like us to talk this through, so that you know where I'm coming from, why I'm saying it, and what you can do to challenge it if you think it's unjust. Let's get it out in the open, and maybe that makes it a bit more trustworthy." There's no way of being a bishop without taking those uncomfortable decisions, but there are ways in which you can try to share the process so as to say, "This is not about me and my power. It is about how I understand what my responsibilities are in this setting, and I want to help you to understand that as fully as possible."

I think back to difficult conversations when I was a diocesan bishop—one with a priest who was in a serious mess in several ways and trying to say, "Look, the basic facts are that the parish is unhappy and you're unhappy. What suggests itself to you in this situation? Because what suggests itself to me is that it's time for you to move on. But not without looking at where the unhappiness is coming from, and also at what might just possibly stop you repeating that cycle somewhere else." Accountability is perhaps trying to make your authority intelligible, making it plain that it is not just about doing things because you can. Augustine as a working bishop knew an enormous amount about that.

Henry Chadwick and Thomas C. Oden

HENRY CHADWICK (1920–2008) was a British theologian and Church of England priest. A leading historian of the early church, Chadwick was appointed Regius Professor at both the universities of Oxford and Cambridge. He was general editor of the Oxford History of the Christian Church, and Oxford Early Christian Texts. His publications included *Origen: Contra Celsum*; *Early Christian Thought and the Classical Tradition*; *Saint Augustine: Confessions* (translation and notes); and *The Early Church* (The Penguin History of the Church).

THOMAS C. ODEN (1931–2016) was an American Methodist theologian, often regarded as the father of the paleo-orthodox theological movement. He was Henry Anson Buttz Professor of Theology at The Theological School, Drew University, and the general editor of the multivolume patristic *Ancient Christian Commentary on Scripture*. The author of numerous books, including a highly regarded three-volume systematic theology, he also served as a general editor for Ancient Christian Texts and as director of the Center for Early African Christianity.

ST. MICHAEL'S ABBEY

Nestled in Southern California's Santiago Canyon, St. Michael's Abbey is regarded as one of the largest communities of the world-wide Norbertine Order. The Abbey's story begins in 1957 when seven Hungarian refugee priests fled from the Communist suppression of their abbey in Csorna, Hungary, and immigrated to Southern California to establish a small monastery in 1961. Today, St. Michael's Abbey has grown to over sixty priests and over forty seminarians in formation. Immersed in a tradition enduring over nine hundred years, the Norbertine Order is named after St. Norbert of Xanten (d. 1134), whose conviction that clerical reform and church renewal were needed in his day through the life and work of monastic communities. St. Augustine of Hippo's rule for clerics, which St. Norbert adopted, continues to be followed among the Norbertines to this day in their communal living and vows of poverty, celibacy, and obedience. St. Michael's Abbey is home to a special collections library that includes papers and fifteen thousand volumes from Henry Chadwick's personal collection, as well as Thomas C. Oden's rare book collection. To learn more about the Abbey, visit stmichaelsabbey.com.

www.ingramcontent.com/pod-product-compliance
Lightning Source LLC
Chambersburg PA
CBHW061810070526
44586CB00024B/2788